T0128564

And I Held Her Hand

A TESTIMONY OF HIS LOVE

LEROY L. MILLER

authorHOUSE®

AuthorHouse™
1663 Liberty Drive
Bloomington, IN 47403
www.authorhouse.com
Phone: 1-800-839-8640

First published by AuthorHouse   11/14//2011

ISBN: 978-1-4678-4542-7 (sc)
ISBN: 978-1-4678-4541-0 (hc)
ISBN: 978-1-4678-4540-3 (e)

Library of Congress Control Number: 2011919737

Printed in the United States of America

Any people depicted in stock imagery provided by Thinkstock are models, and such images are being used for illustrative purposes only. Certain stock imagery © Thinkstock.

This book is printed on acid-free paper.

Sunday Ministries, Inc.
sundayministries@aol.com
AND I HELD HER HAND

Look for other books published through Author House:

"Jimmy Swaggart: The Anointed Cherub That Covereth" (A Catholic Diatribe). A spiritually insightful look into the battle that separated sheep from goats.

"Who Provideth the Raven His Prey?" Poetic writings of a street bound youth who travels from demonic despair to the light that begins to dispel his darkness.

DEDICATION

To my most precious soul mate and friend.
You have been the inspiration for this testimony.
May you continue to bless others from your heavenly outpost
Even as you did while here on earth.
I love you with all of my heart.
I miss you, my Princess.
I'll see you soon.

Contents

FOREWORD

Contained within these pages is a testimony of events that occurred in the lives of two people who fell in love with each other, then with God and then with each other again at a level they did not know was possible. It is my hope that those who find this love will be blessed, encouraged and established more deeply with their God whether they are single or married. I write from actual experiences and make no effort to explain anything to try to sustain someone's existing beliefs. Therefore, if you find yourself challenged by what you read, take it to God to find the truth of it. If it is truth you desire as opposed to confirmation of what you have already decided perhaps you will find it in these pages.

I have prayed for God's guidance and certainly He has brought things back to my memory in vivid detail as my fingers raced across the keyboards trying to type the recounting of events as they flowed into my mind. The foundational principle involved is the unwavering love of God for His people, even when they are struggling to find their way. It is proof of His absolute involvement in the paths of those who open themselves up with a desire to know Him more intimately. He is always there waiting to be invited into every situation. Truly He will direct your path if you are willing to submit yourself to His plan for your life and surrender yourself. Everything else just fans the winds.

I have written through a vale of pain such as I have never known. I have written at the leading of the Holy Spirit. In all that has transpired I have turned to the face of the one I love not understanding all things, but with trust, faith and the great hope He has birthed in me. In the process of this sharing I have again found healing as I recounted the goodness and testimony that He has placed in my life.

I go forward alone carrying within my soul the promises that were given to the two that were one in Him. My course lies before me and I must finish that which I have been given to do. This is my first step into the new unknown that I now walk with my Master who knows the way. With love He shall continue to mark the path until I am called to pass through that same gateway that He took the hand of my Princess and led her through. He has chosen to give her His best much earlier than I wanted Him to, but He knows best. With that and with her, I have trusted Him.

He it is who made footprints in the sand this past season of my life as I fought all of the emotions that come to us when we suffer loss. He took my depression, my anger, my pain, my grief, my loneliness and carried me when I could not get up. Truly He bore my sorrows. He has lovingly continued to direct me toward tomorrow and His promises. What He has spoken He will not fail to perform.

If you need renewal I hope you find it here as I do my best to direct you to Him sharing the experiences of a lifetime. If you are struggling with trust because of difficult circumstances, may you realize from these words that you have someone at the end of your prayers that is worthy of trust. I pray that you will come to know an intimacy with Jesus that will take you to the New Jerusalem and the wedding feast that He has prepared. All who will accept His invitation shall find an eternal relationship of love from the moment you surrender.

Thank you for taking the time to read of the sanctification process that has drawn a man into this love that has overcome his sin and failure. God never quits on you. Don't quit on Him. His mercies are new every morning.

Be blessed.

Chapter 1

IN THE BEGINNING

God works things in us that we don't often understand until we look back from an event that couldn't have taken place if we weren't who He made us to be. Hopefully we were doing what God was directing us to do. Sounds like a lot of nonsense I suppose, but for me the pathway has often involved a step into the unknown….and the more I came to trust God, the more often I had to walk that way. Even some of my early experiences, though I believed in God and had received a calling from Him, were directed by Him without my full knowledge as He took even my missteps and personality quirks to slowly move me to where He wanted me to be.

In my youth I was overwhelmingly shy…something that would keep me in a perpetual state of singleness with few dates until I reached my early twenties. Frankly, this inner shyness has never gone away. I was always so sure of the "turn down" that I locked away the "ask" and never bothered. What few dates I had in high school were arranged by someone else. Of course, I really didn't do myself any favors by greasing my hair straight back to enhance my skinny body, thick glasses and knobby knees. But the good news is we all grow up and out of some of the physical constraints, yet the internalized effects of "fear of failure" can stay with us for a lifetime.

That is where I was at 23 years of age. I had been to college and did get the courage to ask a girl out. She was a beauty and I couldn't believe she said "yes". We dated for three months and I had little understanding of relationships not to mention negligible previous experience that could have helped me in understanding what makes a girl happy. Anyway, I blew that in short order and didn't really date again.

Now I was moving back in with a friend from the first year of college. I was looking for a job and he gave me a place to stay. It is amazing to think that I had somehow stayed connected to this old friend over the previous four years as I finished up college at two other locations, while he finished where we started. But God worked it out that way and His purpose would soon be realized. I wanted to stay in Lincoln, Nebraska, but at the end of three weeks of applying I had hit a dead end. I was packing up to go home and take a job I had been offered in a small town out west. My friend encouraged me to give it one more week. He would spot me what I needed. The first of the following week I found a job and God's plan was in place. My friend became my roommate. I began to meet his friends and their friends. There were a lot of parties and I was always alone.

Some of the "friends" began to recognize my shyness and encouraged me to ask certain girls out, but though I wanted a girlfriend I hadn't encountered anyone I was drawn to. This young lady who was the girlfriend of one of the crew lined me up on a date with one of her friends. I won't go into detail, but it was a fiasco. Yet it was the seed for something greater.

Time passed and summer was coming as was the birthday of the girlfriend's guy. June 4th was a planned celebration day and the girlfriend had a friend returning to town that she was determined to line up with my roommate. He was having nothing to do with it having had the same experience with her "friends" that I had. What can I say? God moved. I hadn't had a date since the fiasco for the usual reason....I never asked anyone. I declared I'd give her another chance, but this was the last time. Really, I wanted a date so badly I could hardly stand it. I was looking for the one for me and I was at the place in life where I just knew she was close by. I just couldn't see her.

The night arrived and I gathered my courage, got in my car and went to the address I was given. My knees were shaking as I stood at the door and knocked. I probably could have gotten an answer without ever touching the door I was so nervous. Then the door opened and there she was. I was so awestruck by her that at first I could not speak. She had to start the conversation and the greeting process. I stumbled through the introduction and escorted her to the car. We spoke quietly and drove to the birthday party.

I was so taken by her that I would find out late in the evening she initially thought I did not like her. As we arrived at the party and walked in she recognized some of her friends and began to converse with them which conversations led her to the kitchen area. She looked back at me. I smiled and told her to go on and visit. I sat on the couch, but I positioned myself so I could see her leaning against the counter in the kitchen. She also watched me and we smiled at one another on occasion. I couldn't move. I was in the state of "I can't believe that this girl is with me!" Finally, my roommate came up to me and gave me a God inspired "pop" on the head. "Hello!" he said. "Have you noticed how beautiful the girl is that you are on a date with? Are you just going to sit here? Get up and get in there and talk to her!" Then he pulled me up by my arm and moved me in the right direction. I managed to get all the way to her, form words and get them out of my mouth.

I discovered she was easy to talk to and I really liked that. The noise of the party had increased in intensity so I asked her if she would like to go for a walk. She was all for it. We exited the front door and began a long, slow walk around a city block as the house was adjacent to a hospital complex and there were no side streets. The block was conveniently and wonderfully long which gave me the time I needed to let myself out of the box. She gave me every indication that she liked me and the conversation. That's when she let me know that she thought I didn't like her because I was so quiet. I made it clear that it was quite the opposite and I was so sorry that I had left that impression. I admitted to my shyness. I would find that she was much like me in that respect. She was surprised to find that I had dated only one other girl more than twice before I met her. Beyond that I could count the number of girls I had been out with without using all of the fingers and thumbs on both hands. She thought I was really cute. (Thank God! She had problems with her vision. I had hope.) Fact is, I knew who I was looking for and I was determined to find her. I had made my case before God, not knowing Him all that well, but I gave Him the criteria anyway.

And here she was! I'm telling you the truth when I tell you that I experienced "love at first sight". By the time we finished that walk around the block I didn't want to share my time with her with anyone else, so I asked her if we could sit on the front porch and just talk. Wow! Where did that courage come from? She was very much in favor of the plan and we made ourselves comfortable on the wide front porch. We never did go back into the party. We talked for hours until it was time to take her home…and I didn't want to. To say we hit it off completely probably doesn't even cover it. She was so gentle in spirit. Her kindness rolled off of her easily touching every aspect of what we talked about. I opened up about myself, as well. She talked freely, but I noticed even then that while she was enjoying our time together, there was an overriding sadness in her eyes that was unmistakable. I wanted to make it go away.

Oh, it was awful! Time had passed and it was time to take her home. Our conversation continued endlessly as I drove continuing even as we sat in front of the house she was renting with some friends. Finally I had to take her to the door. It was late. We stood there in the doorway for a time and I wanted to kiss her so badly. I didn't want to offend her. I didn't want it to be an insignificant peck, either. Somehow I found the right ground and mustered up the courage to give her a kiss that said "I want to see you again" without going over the top. She smiled quite happily and I asked her if I could see her the next day. She said, "Yes." We planned to go to the park. Little did I know at the time all God had in store. He had been working this all along. I did not know that God's plan for our lives would prosper this new love. This gentle, beautiful girl that stood in front of me would touch the depths of my soul and my spirit. I was to know love at a level I did not know existed. She would not just be flesh of my flesh and bone of my bone, but we would be joined together in the Christ that she loved and whom she taught me to love. This love would carry us through every trial and trouble that came our way and we were not exempt from those things. They came along with the moments of great joy. It had begun. I looked into her eyes once more and I thanked God for everything that had transpired up to this time that brought me to this moment before having to tear myself away….and I held her hand.

Chapter 2
THE COURTSHIP

It was a beautiful day at the expansive park. Other friends had joined us at this popular venue. Our day began with a little Frisbee tossing. I found out she wasn't highly coordinated and, at best, was not a runner with her long, skinny legs. She gave it her best shot, but eventually just sat down to watch we boys demonstrate our athleticism. Running after and chucking a Frisbee showed off what I could do. She laughed and enjoyed my antics. That was something I would do from that day forward....clown around, make weird faces, dress funny, show up with my hair done in some strange configuration or tease her in a good natured way which would result in her chasing after me and wrestling me to the ground, floor, bed or couch. Of course I was always a bowl of putty when she caught me and we would laugh together.

As the afternoon wore on I asked if she would like to hit one of the many hiking trails. We wandered off together immediately and the spontaneous sharing that had begun the day before resumed in full force. I could not believe that I had so much to talk about and she enjoyed the fact that I listened so intently to her. Her comment was to the effect "You talk to me like I'm a real person. You don't talk down to me like so many guys do." I attributed that to the fact that when I was a child and there were family gatherings the children were generally shuffled off to another room or the basement, given our food, treats and drinks while being left to play board games or whatever was provided to us. The adults smoked, drank and told stories we weren't allowed to hear in the other area of the house. My brother and I were quite often the only boys. In addition, my Dad worked hard, often long hours, to make ends meet and most of my growing up interactive needs in the conversation realm were held with my mother.

I respected this girl and what she had to say and would always give ear to her in every situation. Demonstrating the initial capability to do that was something she relished. Without realizing it I had gotten something very right that was important to her. She really needed to know that whoever she was with was real and cared for her. I would find out why a little later and discover the reason for the sadness that rested in her eyes even when she smiled or laughed at me.

The summer wore on and we went to our specific jobs each day. She worked for the State of Nebraska as a clerk. Her responsibility was in the driver's license section. She did a lot of filing of completed court actions and mailed the letters out revoking licenses as declared by various courts. I worked at a wholesale heating supply house as a bookkeeper. I spent my days looking forward to closing time. The pathway from my job to her residence got far more action than the one to mine. We had become inseparable, much to the consternation of her roommates. I didn't understand why they were so opposed to her spending so much time with me as we were getting along very well. No one was talking….this time including my constant companion. At one point late in the summer they insisted she go out with them and meet some other guys. She went and told me she was going out with the girls because they thought we were getting too close, things were moving too fast and she had a certain amount of concern over that herself. I was not a happy camper, but I submitted myself to this as there was little I could do to change it. She saw me the next day and told me she had enjoyed a couple of drinks and danced with someone who was at the bar they went to.

I was really upset about it and she saw for the first time the temper that could surface when I felt wronged. She was taken aback by it saying, "You don't own me." I replied, "I know that, but I want to marry you and I don't want you seeing anyone else." Now she was speechless. After a period of silence she said, "You haven't known me that long. You don't know everything that you need to know about me before you can ask that question. I'm not ready to share with you what I will have to share. Please don't be hurt, but, no…I will not marry you." Well, I was hurt. I asked if she wanted to continue seeing me. She said she did. That was the first time we ever parted with negative spirits swirling around us.

I slept, but not well. When I awakened I asked God, who didn't hear from me much unless I was in trouble, what to do. Amazingly, I clearly heard the word flowers. I didn't spare the bucks and I hand delivered a big bouquet of pink flowers (which turned out to be her favorite color) along with a request for forgiveness. I acknowledged that, in fact, I did not own her and I would not force her hand over our relationship, but I wanted more than anything for it to continue. I asked her if she would please not see anyone else for right now while we worked through whatever the issue was that was holding her back and causing her roommates to try to shield her from me. She agreed. It was close to her birthday and I told her I wanted to do something special for her…. whatever she wanted. Frankly, I don't even remember what we did. I just remember that we were together and we were very happy.

I didn't bring up the marriage proposal again though it was never off of my mind. I was absolutely certain of where I stood. There was no doubt in my mind as to the direction I wanted our relationship to take. I had waited a long time to meet this girl and she was everything I had asked God for. I managed to suppress my desire until September when, at the end of a very wonderful evening with all things being at peace, I dared to approach the subject again. Once again she looked into my eyes and said, "No. There is something I must tell you first and I don't know yet how to tell you. When I tell you the story I have to tell you, then you can ask me again if you still want to." I asked, "Is this why you always seem so sad even when we are having a good time together?" She said, "Yes. Because of this I'm not sure I can trust myself to someone. I have been hurt very badly and the hurt is fresh. It just wouldn't be fair to you. But not tonight. I'll tell you when I'm ready." I accepted her declaration that we would get this dealt with whatever it was. I held her close and reassured her that nothing was going to disrupt the love that I felt for her….nothing.

Time continued on and we saw each other every day. I had begun to go to her church with her which pleased her greatly. I had been to that church before as my grandmother always took me when she was visiting when I was a child. It had been my mother's childhood religion, but she had changed when she married my dad. Ironic, I thought, that I was in the reverse position. There was no pressure for me to make any changes in this area, but it actually felt good to be in church every Sunday, especially since I was with my Princess (something I had started to call her which she really liked). September slipped away and fall was upon us. Every day was special to me and I spent them all with her.

October, as it turned out, would be the month when light would be shone on those things that had continued to be shrouded in darkness while our relationship expanded. It was October 7th and the day of reckoning had come. As we sat together outside of her residence in my car I mentioned again that I had not changed my mind about where I wanted our relationship to go. She began to cry and I pulled her even closer. I said, "You surely know by now that you can trust me. You surely know how much I love you. Please trust me with this sadness that eats at you. Please tell me what has happened so we can get it out of the way."

She started slowly, looking deeply into my eyes, and told me that she had been in love before she met me. She was so sure of the commitment that she had allowed herself to become intimate with this man. There was a child. He had turned away from her because his family did not want him to marry someone from her particular religious affiliation. He really didn't care about her at all and it had all been about the physical for him. He bailed.

Left alone to deal with the situation she went to her parents. Her father was more concerned about the embarrassment this was going to cause the family than he was for her mental or emotional wellbeing. He insisted she get an abortion. She refused. She was told she could not stay there. Fortunately, one of the friends she had, with whom she was once again living, made arrangements with her mother in another state so she could stay until the baby was born. During this time she came to the conclusion that she was not emotionally or financially prepared to care for this baby. That is when she did the hardest thing she ever had to do in life. She decided to place the child for adoption.

She wept as she told me and I held her close. (This would be repeated again and again over the next five years as May 2nd rolled around and we acknowledged the birth of this little girl. For the subsequent three years she would just disappear for a good part of the day. I found in something she wrote that it was probably about the fourteenth year when she was able to find peace with God over this lost child, but the pain never left her.) I asked if there was any way we could get the baby back. She said, "No. It is not possible to even know where she is. Besides it would be highly unfair to whoever has her now and has held her in their arms for the past five months to cause them to suffer the same pain I now have to carry."

She looked up at me and my gaze met hers. I was fully engulfed by her pain and I, too, began to weep. When we settled down, I looked into those beautiful, brown, wounded eyes of hers and I said, "I am so sorry that you have had to suffer this terrible hurt and I assure you that I will never do anything to cause you this kind of pain again. It is a hurt I can't fix. But this hurt has brought us together. I would never have wanted you to have suffered this, but because you were abandoned, I found you. I'm so glad he bailed. He is the one who is missing out on a sensitive, beautiful girl. I'm the one who gets to marry her. He loses. I win."

She had a light come into her eyes that overrode the revelation of the moment. "You still want to marry me?" I said, "Will you marry me, my Princess? I'm in love with you. Please don't break my heart by saying 'no' again." She grabbed me around the neck and shouted, "Yes! Yes! Yes, I'll marry you! I love you, too!"

The next months were spent in the joy and work that comes with a "Yes." An engagement ring, wedding rings, invitations, cake selection, wedding dress, tux rental and the whole wonderful, stressful experience was ours to be reveled in. I took classes and joined her church. She was so pleased. To say our relationship deepened would be an understatement. Not yet being in the walk that would eventually encompass us with the Lord, we found we could not contain ourselves before the wedding day. While we had set the date for April, we found one another totally irresistible…something we would take before the Lord in our third year of marriage and ask forgiveness for. As the day drew closer, however, we made a pact, mostly at her insistence that we return to abstinence the last three months before we married even though we had moved in together. She wanted to know that she was more to me than the physical intimacy we had entered into. I reluctantly agreed. I didn't have much choice. She was worth the effort and the wait. I found even more during this time what a great friend she was to have around. We weren't just in love. We were becoming best friends.

The day in April finally arrived and the wedding went off without a single calamity. We had so much fun dancing together, cutting the cake and enjoying our families. We were excited to get started on our honeymoon to Tucson. I think I smiled so hard that night that many of the wrinkles I now have were seared in place to appear later in the furrows that were created.

What joy! What an answer to prayer! I rejoiced in my beautiful bride and I looked into her eyes filled with love for me as were mine for her.... and I held her hand.

Chapter 3
BEFORE THE CHILDREN

As we headed off into wedded bliss it was our mutual desire to put off children for a while though we both wanted them. We felt we needed time just to be us and enjoy married life before introducing a new personality to the mix. With that in mind a visit to the doctor acquainted us with the birth control pill and its use. This would not only turn out to be something we didn't need to do, but something that would give us some regret. But on we went, totally enjoying one another to the exclusion of all outside contact for a while until we decided it was time to rejoin our society of friends.

It is strange how you can slip right back into being a bit of a party guy. You see, that was my calling card. The one who would get a little tipsy and do stuff to make other people laugh. I was always alone, so that was my way of assuaging my loneliness. Did I change personalities when I drank? Yes, I sure did. The quiet, reserved, shy guy got a little crazy when the inhibitions got loosed. My Princess thought it was cute for quite a while until I got a little too crazy one night...a little too drunk. I had never taken a drink before senior year of high school and once I did it took a wrong turn. When I got to college it got way out of hand. It continued to be my internal cover up for fear. Aspects of that were still tagging along with me…aspects that were going to spell trouble down the road a ways.

Time passes so quickly and before we knew it we had experienced nearly two years of married life. From my end everything seemed great. I loved giving her gifts, especially flowers… pink ones. I told her that I loved her all the time and was full of hugs and kisses. What I did not know was that she was completely unused to that kind of attention. In her years of growing up the one thing that plagued her was that she had never had the words "I love you" spoken to her by her parents. The only one who ever said it to her had done so to achieve his purposes as previously stated and then flew the coup. It was becoming clear to her, or so she thought, that my only interest in her was physical and all the gifts and "I love you" expressions had ulterior motives. Along with that she was reaching the point where she wanted to add a new face to our home. She was suddenly not sure if I had any interest in that prospect.

I lost my temper. No excuses. I was offended and lacking completely of any understanding as to where she was coming from. Truth is I was all caught up in how happy I was and did not realize that she was transitioning to another level in our relationship. I provoked her to the point that she said, "I am not a post that you can take out and use whenever you feel the need. I want a divorce."

Whoa! Now I felt like someone had thrust a fire hot iron through my heart. I was getting where she was now and I moved quickly to get us away from that whole area. I asked what I had done that had driven her to this way of thinking. I was incredulous and deeply stupid. I fell back on the one thing that had worked early on….I listened….which I had apparently been failing to do. I certainly had missed all of the signals. I became very quiet. I said, "Don't talk like that. There is no way that I want a divorce. I love you. Whatever I have done or I don't understand, you tell me now. I won't say another word. You talk." And she did.

Talk about an eye opening one way conversation. I was thankful for her gentle nature. She shed some tears, but she did not hold back on the issues that were causing her discomfort with who I was. The drinking was an easy call but it would be another eight years before she got the complete victory on that, though I cleaned up my act. Her father had been a drinker and she had many negative memories of his drinking and his temper. Oh, yes. The temper which I had just exhibited was another negative reminder of the past. When I didn't get my way it had a way of showing up. I was being domineering and I did not even realize it. I had been slowly, and without full knowledge, trying to convert this lady to doing everything my way without regard to the mental anguish and sense of lack of value that I was imposing on her as I did so. I felt like a total heel. It was a good way for me to feel because I was one.

Love conquers all. I apologized and I asked her not to hold back her feelings any more when I did something without thinking. I reviewed her list and moved quickly to pass authority over to her in areas where she felt I was stepping on her toes. She would be willing to listen to my suggestions, but I would be notified without hesitation if I was commanding her to do things my way. Don't get me wrong. This went beyond the aforementioned transgressions. It was about serious stuff like how to fold the towels, or where the dishes should go in the kitchen, which one of us got what drawers in the bureau, which side of the closet was mine, how I wanted my shirts hung up and other critical issues. She was right. I was being very petty. She didn't have to do it the way my Mom did it. It was her house. She loved me enough to hang my shirts according to my desire. Further, we worked out our budget together from then on and decided together on major purchases.

Finally, we discussed the prospect of a new addition. We found we were both ready to proceed and discontinued the birth control. This would bring us to the next hurdle in our lives as a year passed with no results. Coupled with the prior loss of a child this was simply having a devastating effect on my lady. We started researching anything and everything that would create the right mood, zero in on the right time or guarantee victory. All spontaneity went out the window and that began to create frustrations for both of us, but we weren't willing to give up.

During this time she decided that she wanted to do something more with her career since the baby wasn't cooperating. She enrolled in a technical training college for medical assisting. Some of her sisters had gone into nursing, or had other careers, and she felt a little on the outside whenever they got together. The work required was intense and she really poured herself into it. She was determined to make something of herself and needed this sense of accomplishment. This focus allowed for some return to spontaneity but also occupied a great deal of her time for studies. I really encouraged her on this one and I rejoiced with her at her graduation. She was beaming!

Soon after she received a job offer from a local medical clinic and headed off to her new career. She was happy, rehearsing in my ears the events of her days at work. It was here that the doctors would make some effort to help us, but this was not their area of expertise. Since she had a child already the thought was that perhaps I needed a little boost so they tried a hormonal injection. I thought I was going to die. It was worse than the flu when it hit me. I had chills and blankets piled on me with her lying on top of the blankets trying to keep me warm while at the same time I was sweating profusely. I totally soaked out the bedding. It didn't work. We were advised that it might take two or three treatments before we could tell if there was any hope of success. I made it through the second horrendous experience and declared that dead men can't make babies anyway. She was upset but she understood and didn't want me to go through that again either.

At that point we made the decision to adopt. Nothing had worked and there seemed to be no hope for us. We were told that we simply could not have children. That was a hurt that I did not expect. It was a crushing revelation for my wife. We contacted the same service she had used when she had proceeded with the adoption already spoken of. The waiting list was a year if we would accept a mixed race or alternate race child. We did not think at the time that a child of another race would gain acceptance by her parents. This would not be fair to the child. The waiting list for a Caucasian child was forever. Once again we were despondent.

We began to turn more to God as these issues crowded in destroying the life we had planned for ourselves. We fell in with folks at our church that directed us to some weekend retreats. They were some born again believers we would find out. The retreats would help us deal with our life's issues by helping us learn to inject God into our lives.

I went fighting and kicking all the way. This bubbly, happy fellow took me under his wing and wouldn't let go. I began to relax with the cot, the gym, the lack of privacy and the early rah-rah shout with follow up rousing song at an ungodly hour of the morning. Some of what was being said soaked in and touched that place in my heart that reminded me that I had a clear call to ministry when I was fourteen. I had run away from it encouraged that I had done the right thing after a confrontation with a pastor from my old church that resulted in my dad physically removing him from our home.

Here I was isolated with the one who had once touched me…the one that I had a casual "I'll call you when I need you" relationship with. After much sharing, much testimony of lives changed and bible study we were given an opportunity to go to an assigned room by ourselves for prayer and consideration of all that had been presented to us. While in that room, I found myself opening up to God the way I had opened up to my wife on that night we met. The honesty that I was able to express about myself…the good, the bad and the ugly….and my hurts began to break loose some hidden away pain. Suddenly I realized I was not alone in that room any more as I was engulfed in a cloud (spiritual, not literal) of peace I had never experienced. I was so comforted that I began to weep asking for forgiveness and for changes to be made in my life. I was happy with my wife, but I was not happy with myself or nearly as confident and settled as everyone thought I was. I came out of that room a changed man with a lot of changes that would stem from this initial experience over the coming years. My darling wife was blessed in the same way when she attended with the women the next month. We were a changed couple. We had been going to church for a long time, but now we had received the gift of Jesus Christ on a personal basis making Him Lord of our lives.

We made a commitment to God at this time. We brought repentance for previous actions before Him and we walked away feeling that we were set free. The ultimate proof would come through the ensuing years when we were blessed in so many ways as we learned to follow His will and His way.

Yes. He heard our cry. It took a year or so, but when it looked like even adoption was a door closed to us and we would be a childless couple, we still rejoiced in each other and the new kind of love that was happening to us. My wife's boss called her into his office at the end of the work day and told her that a young girl that he was caring for had asked him to find a couple for her child. She was going to give the baby up for adoption. Would we be interested?

I came home from work to an ecstatic lady who grabbed me and danced me around the room. She was shouting praise to God. We were going to have a baby after all! As the initial shock wore off I danced her around and we both shouted! We were new to God's workings but we knew He had a full hand in what had just taken place. The impossible had just become possible! We were going to be parents! The desire to go to school, the office she was hired to work in, involving her boss and co-workers in our struggles and ultimate disappointments were all part of God's design for what He was doing now. We would be able to provide a good home to a child and offer assurance through her employer to the young lady that her baby would be loved. God had returned what had been lost. We sat for a long time with what was now God's new reality for our lives….and I held her hand.

Chapter 4

NEW ARRIVALS

The coming days were spent with great joy. I tagged along whenever I could to join in the shopping and preparation for the arrival of our little bundle of joy. There was the baby bed to buy, baby clothes, stocking up on diapers (these were the old days so they were cloth with plastic pants...I would soon know the joys of squeezing out diapers so I could throw them in the washer), safety pins, sheets, baby bed decorations and room decorations. It was made all the more fun because we had recently moved to our first home and we bought it new. It was small but more than adequate for a couple with one child.

The days passed so slowly. The due date was originally thought to be around Christmas to the first of the year. They didn't pinpoint things then like they do now. Christmas came and went. The New Year celebration came and went. Fear tried to come on us that something had gone wrong. But the little guy, whom we now knew would be a boy, was just taking his time. It was a good thing it was a boy because we had a name but had never been able to settle on a name for a girl. Finally, on January 11, 1979 we received a call that our son had been born. He weighed in at 10 pounds 6 ounces. I thought, "Was this boy born at Christmas and they just didn't tell us until now? Good grief. He's already as big as I am."

There would now be a three day agonizing wait before we would be escorted to the hospital by the attorney to pick up our boy. We inadvertently got on the elevator with the attorney and when the doors slid open on the floor where the baby was a very knowing nurse grabbed us immediately and shoved us back into the elevator saying, "No. No. No. You wait downstairs. You are not supposed to be up here." We apologized but could not stop smiling. Soon, just as she said, that same nurse…this time beaming a great big smile…walked up to us with the attorney. She had a big bundle of hospital blankets in her arms. She laid down the baby boy and rolled back the blankets for us to see him. Wow!! He looked like someone had "whopped" him with a stick about the head and shoulders. But he was beautiful! The nurse commented that he had a tough delivery because he was so big. He still had forceps marks all over his head with the associated bruising as well as a good deal of puffiness in his face and around his eyes. And was he ever big! My wife asked if the mommy was ok. We received a "Yes, but she was mighty sore." Then we bundled up our baby in the blankets we had brought and headed out into the -15 degree F. weather, ice and snow to escort him home. I still have the picture that was taken immediately after we laid him on our bed. We stood there what seemed like forever just looking at him sleeping. It would be six months before the final decree that would make him ours.

I continued working and the new Mom took a leave of absence to stay with our new arrival for about three months. Then it was back to work for her and daycare services for him. I was becoming increasingly unhappy with my job and I had always wanted to move south. I hated the winters and we had just been through a rough one. But before we got away I became aware that a girl who worked in my office and her husband were going through the same agonizing pain of wanting to start a family without success. They had found this doctor who specialized in fertility who discovered she had endometriosis, which was far more common than we knew. She had surgery to clean out her tubes and became pregnant.

My wife immediately scheduled an appointment with the same doctor. Meanwhile, she insisted I get checked on my count…something that had never been done. To say the least I was embarrassed by the entire procedure, especially since I had to go to her office for the test where everyone knew us and tolerate the snickers. Lo and behold, I had no count. I was referred to a specialist who quickly ascertained that an old grade school injury, which I remember having been taken to the doctor for, was causing the problem. It was a varicocele and the blood circulation through that was killing all of the sperm. He told me it would have to be fixed before I got too much older or it would cause me a great deal of discomfort due to the weight. It would certainly change things with respect to pregnancy capabilities. So, off I went to surgery. I would soon be able to tell you in advance of any weather changes for approximately a year.

Meantime, my wife determined that she was going to proceed with her appointment with her specialist. Though my results were outstanding, which results were obtained through another humiliating journey to a different testing station, she had this sense that it had to be done. I'm so glad she made that decision. It turned out that she had an unusual tilt to her uterus after the doctor went in through her belly button and scoped everything out. Though she had a child, ensuing monthly cycles and not having cycles due to the birth control pills had caused a "layering" or building up of tissues around the end of her tubes. She had endometriosis, too. The doctor stated, "If it's hot outside and you can get a cold drink across the street, you're not going to drive clear across town to get one." Bottom line was that as the eggs would travel down the tube they found the tissue build up to be quite suitable and snuggled in right there. The doctor said he needed to clean up the mess and cut loose the uterus to reposition it better so it wouldn't happen again. Then she could carry a baby better. "We've got to get those little buggers down there where you can get at them," he said. Now we had more understanding of the unusual pain she also went through during each cycle. Things got worse with each one because her body could not cleanse itself. We had renewed hope and an answer that suggested that our child would not be an only child.

The surgeries were now behind us and we moved off to Oklahoma. We had prayed about it and decided to sign the papers on our little house and put it up for sale. If it sold, we went. If not, we stayed. We signed on Friday and went to visit her parents. Sunday night when we returned the realtor had an offer on the house. Monday it was sold.

My wife was hired on at another medical clinic in Edmond,

Oklahoma. I had previously applied to a temperature controls company and been hired tentative to our house selling. We had a nice home and life was good. We had a great church of our religious affiliation nearby that was even more dynamic than the one we had come from. It was alive. I was able to continue my golf habit on a local course. My sister lived in Moore with her family so we had some family in proximity and we got together from time to time. The fall of 1980 turned into winter with no visible signs of new additions. The doctor had said it could take a while to heal and for everything to click. It did. It would be the spring of 1981 when my wife would begin to have funny feelings. She was excited, but almost afraid to hope for what might be. The doctors at her office ran the test and we killed the bunny rabbit! You couldn't have gotten us down off the ceiling with ten big guys and a good rope!

The time to assert self also arrived for my wife. When we named our first son she indicated she was fond of the name Joshua and that God had indicated to her that she would have a son who would bear that name. With all of the negative news about our capabilities to have children she had thought to use the name on our first child. I was adamantly opposed to the name. I don't know why. I just was…and I stood my ground. Eventually God brought us to agreement on the name Aaron, so Joshua was still open. She made it clear this would be his name.

By this time the opposition I had to this name had turned more positive…I suppose because I was becoming more deeply religious and I was also getting more used to these leadings from the Lord. However, not being totally submitted to this direction yet, I told her I was going to pick the middle name just in case our child didn't like it. He would have a backup name. Oh, yes. She absolutely knew it was a boy from the beginning. Once again we could not settle on a girl's name. After much thought I determined that Joshua's middle name would be Michael. This was a name that was in my family and I liked it. She liked it, too. So it was settled…or so I thought. I was about to have one of those dreams that I had begun experiencing that were so vivid and often carried direction.

The dream took me through the entire birthing process which was something I had never been through. I was taking classes with my wife though and I was the designated coach for the delivery. To say I was scared doesn't cover it. I would be there to witness the birth of our son.

The dream I had went amazingly like the actual events. Our son was born and in the dream the doctor held him up to me in both hands saying, "You have a fine son. What will his name be?" I replied, "His name is Joshua Michael." Suddenly a firm hand rested on my shoulder and a deep, powerful voice said, "No! His name will be Joshua James!" I woke up, woke my wife up, told her the dream and she said, "And…" I said, "And his name is Joshua James." And it is. In the actual birth the doctor laid Joshua on my wife's tummy and said, "What's his name?" Close enough.

What a joy to bring home another child! My wife was so happy to have this child of promise for whom she had been given a name so many years before. This was what she held on to. God gave her a name and told her she would have a son. Despite all the negative reports, she believed that it would someday happen though she had that moment of doubt when Aaron first came along and thought to use the name. God used my stubborn nature to His advantage to keep that from transpiring. You see God said to her, "You will have a son…."

My wife suffered from some postpartum and was very tired. This baby logged in at 9 pounds 6 ounces. We didn't know what a little baby looked like. He had come in rather quickly on January 21, 1982. I remember being so tired in the early morning hours from coaching breathing that I sat in a chair next to the hospital bed, leaned forward with my head against the edge of the bed and went to sleep. I got my little cat nap in preparation for the next contraction. We went from 4 or 5 centimeters of dilation through two hard contractions and we were on our way to delivery at full dilation with all systems go. It was amazing to see my son come into the world.

The postpartum brought memories of a child given away. My Princess was having trouble dealing with it again and felt that she was so unworthy to be a mother. I tried to tell her that God had already declared her worthy when He told her about Joshua and gave her the name. She was still sure she was doing a terrible job. That simply wasn't true in any respect. Where she thought she was impatient, I saw a woman of great patience, and so on. I knew what impatient looked like because he looked at me in the mirror every morning. It was determined by her that she needed a fresh ear…someone whom she could be open with about her feelings and this time I had to take a back seat. Whomever she went to it was ordained of God. The counseling brought her around to a better view of herself. Postpartum depression was behind her. That made me happy as well.

The years of trying to have babies without success were over. What we did not realize was that we were in a whole new realm with respect to our intimate interaction. Everything was functional. The targets were taking their position and the ammo was now live. Way too soon we discovered we were pregnant again. Having tried so long to get where we now were had not prepared us for "you need to mark the time and be careful." This time we were shocked and still trying to learn to juggle the demands of a three year old with the demands of a new baby. And the three year old was not into sharing time. My wife actually cried as this was still in the window of time for shaking off the depression that she was experiencing. Her body and emotions had simply not recovered enough. She struggled the next eight weeks with various physical problems. One morning as I prepared to go to work, she indicated she simply could not get out of bed. I said I had to go to work for a while but I'd be back as quickly as I could. I took care of the boys needs and asked the neighbor to check in on her. She came back and forth checking on the boys and did spend time there. I went to work but I would feel guilty about this choice for years to come.

I had gotten home and was preparing dinner. My wife was resting in our bed and I checked on her frequently. Suddenly she began screaming, crying and calling my name. I raced into the room and asked her what was wrong. She was extremely emotional and shouted, "I just lost the baby!" I jerked back the covers expecting to see the worst and there was nothing. Immediately I thought she had perhaps dozed off and had a dream. I said, "Princess, you are ok. There is nothing here." She became very agitated with me and said emphatically, "The baby is gone! Help me get to the bathroom!" I helped her out of the bed and moved her to the toilet where everything suddenly happened. I called the hospital and they said to bring the placenta and other remains so they could determine if they had to do a D and C to be sure everything came out. I got a plastic bag and fished around in the toilet until I recovered all that was there. I was completely shaken. We rushed to the hospital after I got the boys to the neighbors. They examined everything there and sent us home after a few hours indicating that my wife should continue to rest but that no further procedure was necessary.

Once home, we finally grasped what had just taken place and we wept in each other's arms. The neighbors kept our boys for the night and we slept fleetingly. This would be the beginning of the end for my tenure at my job. I had placed my fear of my superior and his attitude over the well -being of my wife and family. That wouldn't happen again.

The next morning, as things began to play back in my mind, I came to the question of how my wife had known it was over before it was over. So I asked. She said, "You probably won't believe me." I said, "Tell me." As she was lying in bed she had a sharp twinge in her abdomen and then noticed a mist form on her belly. The mist slowly rose through the room to the ceiling area and then passed out of sight. She knew it was the spirit of our child and when she asked God in that moment He let her know that she (yes, it was a girl) was not strong enough to make it and He had taken her home.

My wife felt guilty that she had feelings of not wanting this child and I was devastated by my lack of priorities. The fact that I had left my precious wife alone in this situation with a little boy and a baby was going to be weight on my shoulders. It would be five years later as I knelt in an altar once again weeping over my guilt that God would finally touch me and set me free from this burden I carried. In that moment of remorse, He opened my eyes to a vision of a beautiful little girl in a white lacy dress whose head came to the waist area of the one standing behind her with his hands on her shoulders. She looked to be about five years old....the age our daughter would have been. The one standing there said, "Why do you grieve? Do you not know that she is with me?" Then I really cried...this time for joy.

My wife found her healing from God much sooner than I did. In her agony He also spoke to her a very short time later. He did not address her feelings of guilt, but simply said, "You will have another son and you will name him Jonathan." He then proceeded to show her exactly what type of boy he would be from a personality standpoint....and he has been all that was declared. What a merciful God we serve!

I returned to the hospital a day later and asked to have the remains of our child given to us so we could hold a memorial service with a burial.

I could not believe the harshness of the response I received from the nurse. "Oh, my god! It was just a bunch of tissue! We threw it all away! There is nothing you can do about it." We had our memorial service at church without the remains and there would be no burial.

The pain of the latter part of 1982 passed with time and we wrapped ourselves around the promise God had given with joyful expectation. Early in 1983 we got the news. Jonathan was on the way. We didn't need anyone to tell us if it was a boy or a girl. We already knew. He would be born November 2, 1983 in a delivery room that was shrouded in plastic to protect it from adjacent construction. What a wild scene played out that day! This little one didn't wait long after our arrival at the hospital to make his appearance. I was again coaching my wife and was present when the nurse came in to check her dilation. She was having some hard contractions and the nurse found her to be at 5 centimeters. A flag went up in my head and I asked the nurse to call the doctor. She scoffed at me and said we were hours away from that. I said, "You don't understand. I've been through this. We're going to need the doctor shortly." She waved her hand in the air and muttered something unintelligible as she went out the door.

Within five minutes we hit two successive very hard contractions. My wife yelled, "Jonathan is coming out!" I looked and she was absolutely right. I shouted, "Hang on! I'll get the nurse!" I ran into the hallway and there was no one to be found. I ran down the hall to the nurses' station...void. I ran over to the other hallway (it had the usual 'H' pattern) and spotted my skeptic clear down at one end. I shouted for her to come. The baby was coming. She walked toward me in a very frustrated manner making mention that she had other duties and I need not be a nuisance. I ran in place next to her trying to exhort her to hurry. As we got closer to the room she heard my wife and picked up the pace a little. She entered the room and looking at me with absolute incredulity pulled back the sheets in a manner that was intended to let me know I was an idiot. The sheet drew back and revealed....a shout from a shocked nurse! "Don't push! Don't push! Hold him back! We'll get you to the delivery room!" She had some sort of radio on her and the next thing I knew people materialized out of nowhere. The nurse literally threw my hospital garb into my face and said, "Hurry up and get dressed if you want to see this baby born!" The doctor had been called and, while he was 15 minutes away legally, he ran two red lights and got to the delivery room at the same time I did. I had run into the bathroom to get my stuff on and as I came out I received a healthy pop on the head as the door flew back into me because my wife and her bed were passing by.

I delayed for a moment because I had forgotten my booties and tried it again…hopping on one foot down the hallway trying to get the last booty on. There was no one to be seen anywhere. I was looking all over and finally found a nurse at the nurses' station. All I could get out was, "Which way did they go? Which way did they go?" I was directed through the plastic curtain and found my way to the delivery room. The doctor was running in the opposite door with his arms out as a nurse on either side held his gown for him to run into. He took one look and said, "Not yet! Hold him back!"….to which my wife responded, "You have got to be kidding! My whole bottom is falling off!" Two pushes and we were parents again. Jonathan weighed in at 9 pounds 4 ounces. So much for little babies, I thought. I looked at my wife and said, "You were all baby again. I can't believe you have had such big babies."

Here we were. We had three little boys that were under the age of 5. While we talked about the desire to have a little girl, we ultimately determined that this was it for us. Necessary steps would have to be taken and an arms ban was to be imposed. It was just a matter of who would get the short straw. My Princess looked at me with those big browns noting that she had now been through four pregnancies, three deliveries, a miscarriage and surgery. Yes. I got the short straw.

As usual, I had the joy of being scheduled for an office procedure with all the folks we had come to know and love that my wife had worked with. By now she was at home working as a homemaker. And everyone knew what I was there for. The snickering was delightful. I was escorted to the room of my manly demise, inoculated with some valium (thank God), stripped from the waist down and mounted on a table of affliction. Let's just say that every hidden thing was now revealed and exposed to the light. The doctor came in and announced that there was a student nurse or two in the building and he would very much like to have them witness this procedure. I should have known. I'd been set up. This really wasn't free. There was a price. I just hadn't been informed of all of the details of my lovely spouse's negotiations.

My wife smiled at me...oh, yes...she knew. "It's for medical training, Sweetie," she said. I said, "Ok." The valium was making me real relaxed. The door to the room opened and in strode the student nurses all giggling. Not one or two....eight. Then all of my wife's fellow employees joined the group. I couldn't believe it!

The doctor started the procedure and joyfully pulled this tube way up where I could see it and clipped it. I almost passed out. All of my witnesses started giggling again. The door opened again and someone shouted to the doctor, "Mrs. So and So is at the hospital in delivery and you are needed now!" He looked at me and said, "Got to go. The other doctor will be in shortly to finish you up." I got a glimpse of eternity lying there on my pedestals with the whole world watching. Soon the other doctor came in and it was over. I looked at my wife who was caught up in the humor of the situation and stated, "You owe me."

There we were. We were a happy family of five living the middle class life. It was all to the good. God had done all He said He would do. He was with us every step of the way and I'm sure He had some good laughs over how it all transpired, too. We had three little boys. Wow! We were so proud. We often stood, her head on my shoulder, looking at them in their little beds sleeping...and I held her hand.

Chapter 5

COMFORT ZONES BEGIN TO UNRAVEL

It was 1983 and I had changed companies, though I was still involved in the same line of work. Several people had left the company I was with for the same reason and one in particular who had taken me under his wing was at the competitive company. He talked me into joining their new team. This would be a tool used by the Lord to take me to the next step. I did not know that the economic situation in Oklahoma was going to become difficult and this start up by the company I joined would be short lived.

As 1984 rolled around it became clear to me that things were not going to go well. Two mechanics and I took a serious look at starting off on our own, but ultimately found this to be an unrealistic venture with no capitalization available. My wife and I were faced with a huge dilemma. I was out of work with nothing on the horizon. We prayed. Before my final day at this company I was contacted by a salesman from back in my Nebraska wholesaling days who had been instrumental in helping me get hired by the first company I had been with in Oklahoma. He was aware of a position in Wichita, Kansas and suggested that I apply. He was sure I'd be a perfect fit.

While we were not in any position to make that kind of a move, nor did we desire to, there was no other door open to us. I made the drive up to Wichita and went through the application and interview process. For the next six weeks, I was provided a very nice place to stay in Wichita during the week while I worked at this new job and commuted on the weekends to be with my family. I began looking for a place to live, but could not get my home sold in Edmond due to the economy.

One of the mechanics that I had worked closely with became aware of our situation and, while he would have preferred to live towards the city, rented our home indicating we could keep it up for sale and he would move out once it sold. Praise God! We would be back together and the house would be secure. Now I searched in earnest for a home around Wichita finally settling on a home in Rose Hill. It was a great deal. The airline industry was struggling and home values were also down there. People had to move on leaving a lot of vacant homes. I plunged ahead without asking God for His input. We were soon moving into a lovely home in a rural neighborhood. Prior to leaving we would visit with our pastor at our present church to let him know what had transpired and that we would have to move on. We were pretty involved in activities at the church and wanted to say our good-bye. I was amazed when he sat back and said, "I must warn you about where you are going. You will find that it is dead and dried up compared to what you are used to. Your faith will be tested. Try to hold on to what you have found here."

Whoa! Now that was a message of impending doom I hadn't expected, particularly regarding my religious connections. My wife and I put that on the "thinking" shelf and went ahead with the only way out we were provided. God was about to shake up our world and we didn't know it.

As we settled in and got our oldest enrolled in Kindergarten we began to enjoy our surroundings, meet the neighbors, etc. From the very first week we discovered we would be in for a bit of a drive to attend the church of our denominational persuasion. Once located, we made our first joyful trip to the facility that was always the high point of our week. Sundays were great and we always left inspired. Not this day. The ominous message we had received bore full fruit. It had been right on. We both walked out of the service and looked at each other. There was nothing. It had been awful. This would continue for a number of weeks as we remained faithful to the Lord and the practices we had learned. During one service a lady came up flooded with tears to where we were positioned at the back so we could have our own little praise service without bothering anyone else and asked if she could join us. She joined hands with us and the three of us worshipped together as we had done at our prior church. It made her quite happy.

However, God was not going to let this continue. I walked out of a service one day and said (rather loudly), "I feel like I just attended a funeral service for twelve people!" to which my wife responded with a quick "Hush, people hear you." Yes, they did. The people in the parking lot had turned to look at me. I could not do it anymore. Neither could my wife. She met a lady that she commiserated with about our situation and the hunger she had to go back where we were. This lady wisely informed her that it sounded like God was taking us forward to something new and asked if she would attend a Women's Aglow meeting with her. My wife accepted having no idea what this was. She would attend their next gathering.

In the meantime, I was busying myself with anything I could on Sunday mornings so I could skip the service. The high point of my week had become the low point and I didn't want to face the rest of my week that way again. I began watching television, surfing the channels to find something to lock into so I could excuse myself from going to church. My wife dutifully continued to attend. I stayed home. During one of these home "surfing" modes I happened upon a preacher that was pointing his finger at me and made a comment that I found irritating (later that word would change to convicting). I jumped up to change the channel (remember, I'm old and there were no remotes that I had access to during this archaic age) stating that I wasn't going to listen to that garbage. Having spoken this out loud I was stunned to hear an audible voice respond to me as I returned to my chair....."Turn it back for he has words that I would have you hear!" It was firm and it was as the sound of a mighty wind. I was completely shaken never having had this experience before while awake. With shaking hands I returned to the television and put it back on the channel I had moved away from. From then on I would watch this preacher absorbed by the gospel being presented in a manner I had never before heard it. This was the point at which I actually picked my bible back up and started to read for myself what it said. And that had been the challenge this man had given me that day. Since, I have read through it numerous times, studying and receiving the depth of its message into my heart. I would always make sure that whoever was preaching to me was coming out of the foundational truths revealed to me by God's spirit that are contained therein.

My wife had gone on to attend the meeting she was invited to. She found it to be a quite different experience but was hungry for the freedom she found these people to be worshipping God with. It was a revelation experience for her to see so many women focused on God and she began to participate by opening herself up to worship as those around her were doing. There was a message followed by people getting in line to be prayed for. Being a dutiful young lady from a background that would on occasion have such a line, she got in it to go up and get blessed. As she reached the front of the line and stepped forward for her blessing, the lady doing the praying reached out to touch her head and that is the last thing she remembered for a while. The power of the Spirit of God hit her hungry spot and she went crashing to the floor....totally unharmed physically....but unable to move under the power that had hit her. When she was able to get up the change that had taken place at that weekend meeting years before was magnified by what had just happened inside her. She was filled with outward praise for God that came from an inward bubbling that she could not contain.

My wife walked in the door from that meeting and she was no longer the woman I had married. I recognized in a moment's time that she was carrying a joy that I had never seen in her in the happiest of times. It would so permeate her that I became hungry for whatever it was that she had. At her insistence, we visited a different church that turned out to be "Pentecostal" in structure. We weren't quite ready for the goings on we experienced and, frankly, witnessed some things that I would later discover were manmade abuses of the gifts God gives. From this day forward the Lord would take us from place to place showing me what His word declared, where He was pleased with the activities and where the traditions and teachings of doctrines of men had circumvented His Word and Spirit, much like the Israelites were in the habit of doing.

This new journey had locked itself in place in our lives. We would soon discover that our lives were not our own. We were on a course that was established for us and we had little choice but to follow as doors closed and only one door would open which we had to go through. But while it would be fraught with trials and hardships at times, we grew in the assurance as these times came and went that we were not alone. We both began to experience inner workings that came forth in dreams and visions that we had to submit ourselves to and receive direction from. This direction was always fully in line with God's word. Much was explained to us by those far more familiar with what was happening to us than we were. We were fortunate to be where we were.

The time for us to be in this place ended as the first year was drawing to a close. This was not good. The real estate market had gotten worse and the parameters of my job description were going to change to the point that I knew with certainty we were going to go under. It became quite strong in my spirit that we needed to reconnect with our roots in Lincoln, Nebraska. I had not really left there on good terms and I did not realize at the time that God was taking me back to deal with my failures and bitterness. At the same time I would come to the place where I could receive what my wife had. I didn't know why I couldn't get what she had, but God did. It had to be dealt with as it was the wall that held back His blessing.

It was hard for me to call the person that was actually the source of my bitterness. Once again, that same salesman was involved and had communicated my newfound capabilities to those I had worked with years before. He also let them know that things weren't working out where I was and I was looking. He told me to call. I did. There was a meeting with the individual I spoke of and it went quite well. I apologized for prior years actions and he apologized for what he had done. We hit if off really well and determined that we would go forward together in business. I found that he had also had a change in religious affiliation brought about by a divorce and we would find our new church (Pentecostal orientation) through him, as well. God was continuing our training.

Things up to this point had continued the unraveling of our comfort levels from a physical standpoint. Talk about needing God to intervene... we were in a situation of His making and He was the only way out. We turned to Him more than ever. We now owned a house in Oklahoma, a devalued home in Kansas and we were trying to move to Nebraska.

Help, God! I again began weekly commutes that would last six weeks while my resurrected company put me up in a nice suite during the week and I drove the five hours one way home Friday nights with the return trip late on Sundays.

While in Lincoln, I began to look for a place for us. That was faith. I had no money and already owned two homes I couldn't sell. I spoke with my wife daily and she began to use that gift that had surfaced in her during the past year as she directed me in finding the house we would have. She saw a map and described it to me over the phone. I pulled out a phone book in my room and was amazed to see what she was describing. She said, "There are two major lines and they cross. Where they cross you need to begin looking to the left of this line and below this line. You are looking for a green colored house that is two levels. When you walk in the door there will be steps going up and down. There will be a door. You will go out to a patio area and there will be something over your head." Wow! This was new. I had been working with a real estate lady and I gave her the information. She was truly puzzled, but said she had two houses that met that description in the designated area. She drove me to the first house and as we pulled up to the curb I said, "This is not it." She said, "It is green and it has two stories. Don't you want to look at it?" "No," I said. "This is not it. Take me to the other house." How I knew that I do not know, but I just knew. I was learning about that "connection" God will give you when you are on target. We drove to the second home, again pulling up to the curb and my spirit quickened within me.

We walked in the front door and there were steps going up to the main house and steps going down to the basement. I began to go up the steps to the living room which had a railing adjacent to the steps. As I moved up and looked to my left I saw the duplicate of our couch sitting against the far wall. I stopped cold for a few moments as what was happening began to grasp me fully. Remembering what had been said, I requested to go back down and see the basement first. It was nicely finished and as I moved through I saw a back door which I went to and proceeded outside. Once there I realized that there was a full wood deck over my head with the patio that I was standing on under it. This was the house my wife saw.

In conversations with the owner, I was to find through the real estate agent that they owned the place and had built a new home that they were anxious to move into. As I said, I had no money and two homes tied up. They told us to move in for minimal rent so the house was occupied and they would carry a note for us until we could get our other homes sold. God was at work! We were both overjoyed that our separation would once again be coming to an end. It had been hard. As we focused on this new move I came to the place where I had only one payment left on the Kansas house and we would be facing bankruptcy and foreclosure. I distinctly received direction to take this money and give it to the preacher that I had been watching on TV on a regular basis. I was not fully submitted and unsure of what I had just heard so I said, "Lord, if this is you, then you sell our house for us and I'll give the money." Not full faith, but God would honor this fleece I had put out and I would have a contract on the house in three days. Remember that I bought it without consulting God and, while He definitely put us where we were, my error would cost me. I lost $15,000 dollars on the deal, $5,000 of which I had to borrow from my Dad to close on the house and pay my way out. Within 30 days, as I recall, God went a step further and sold our house in Oklahoma. He did more than I asked. I sent the money as directed. My wife was in full agreement. Fact is she was so sure it was from God she said, "Send it. We can't save ourselves with it."

We settled into our new home with a new loan and contract. I began repainting it right away as I was forever fixing on any home we had. The kids were in school and we praised God that we were home. We were once again comfortable and happy. We found our new church and began to experience more growth in our spiritual lives even as I faced my sins and failures from our previous life there. I did all I could do to make things right...requesting forgiveness where necessary.

It was this process that finally opened the door to fill the hunger I had inside me to receive that which was working so powerfully in my wife. She had grown marvelously strong without losing her wonderful, compassionate, gentle nature that I so loved. But I had to be freed from my past even as she had been. It's just that mine was so hidden away that I did not know it was there (and the part I knew about I didn't want to talk about). It just reared its ugly head every now and then which I would give a quick, "that's just who I am.....I wish I could change" response to. I was ashamed of my failures but seemingly helpless when the temptation came. The church had some counseling sessions that dealt with the spiritual side of who we were that also would search you out to help you find the reasons behind negative physical outward actions. It was here one night that, as I took my turn voluntarily in the chair, I found again that place where I could open up and expose the wounds that were hidden away. The sinful behaviors that had been used in my life which I had begun to practice and be involved in were revealed to me. I had forgotten about the incidents but the seeds of those things were still there producing bitter fruit. I'm not sure exactly what happened but the willingness to express these painful and ugly truths about my inner most being sent a flood that I could feel all through me as those around me prayed for my deliverance from past hurts. I felt the Spirit of God go into those places and clean them out replacing them with Himself. As the saying goes, "I was set free!" I would learn as life went on that while I was free, it was an area of weakness that Satan himself would try time and again to push the button on to turn me away from God during the trials and tribulations that would come. He never quits trying. He never comes at you where you are strong. This knowledge would give me great compassion for those in similar struggles in the future. I would find that God's grace had a keeping power to it, not just one of mercy.

These same folks became aware of my desire to be "filled with the Spirit" as my wife had been so I'd have that overcoming power working in me that I saw in her. Every method was tried. The old "Dutch rub", the "push him down", the "shout in his ear" until he gets it, and so on. I'm not trying to be picky, but honestly, if you want it you will get it … in God's time…when He sees you are ready. My house (temple) was still undergoing some reconstruction. The day came, however, when I was all alone. I was in my oldest son's room who knew no fear of anything, but in this new house he would not go into his room alone. I was there with him but had dozed off awakening at 2:30 in the morning not having returned to my own bed. As I awoke, a power went all through my body and I sat straight up speaking for several moments in what I knew to be fluent German. I was raised listening to my German family speak it around the table so I was fully familiar with it. I would not speak it again as the language changed and would only appear from time to time when in deep prayer with the Lord. Everything I had hungered for began to happen for me as I saw it occurring in my wife. I had strength in me I had never felt before. The eyes of love that I had for my wife began to encompass my soul and my spirit.

This baptism would actually be both wonderful and a curse. I began to receive knowledge of things I did not know with words of correction, exhortation, encouragement, and so forth. I knew in my spirit that I was to write them down. I did. Not understanding them, I would go to my pastor asking him what they meant not being fully "educated" yet on biblical things. He had been withdrawn from me since my session in the chair and now he actually tended to take some of what was written personally responding with verbal anger, which I did not understand. He became more of an adversary in coming months.

It was during this time that another individual took me under his wing being aware of the gift that was being stirred up in me. As we sat visiting one day I mentioned to him that I had spoken something in the middle of the night. He asked me what it was and I told him. He looked astonished. He asked me, "Do you not know where that is recorded?" I said, "No." Please understand that I was still in the initial stages of wrestling my way through the Old Covenant section of my bible. He turned to the New Covenant to the Gospel of John. I had just quoted John, chapter one and verse one to him.

My wife and I also became aware that something was very wrong in the house we were in. One night a light in the living room turned on after we had gone to bed. I remember slowly moving down the hallway with some weapon I had picked up scared to death to find a lamp burning but no one in the house. I thought a bulb was loose or something, but no amount of shaking the lamp or the plug could duplicate the event. Later, as I prepared to go on a sales trip, I walked into the living room and the heavy set of drapes over the picture window opened on their own about a foot. Again, this could not be duplicated. A little later my wife would hear the front door open as she was giving the boys baths. She called my name thinking I had come home from my road trip. She then heard the sound of steps going to the basement and running to the back door. She would find both doors open. We told folks at church and they came to pray. We were having a new experience. We would be used this way to help others. Finally, it was after a rather rough storm which found all of our sons gathered in bed with us, that my wife and I moved to Aaron's room rather than moving all of the boys back to their beds. Here we would come face to face with what was lurking in our midst.

After sleeping a couple of hours I came under attack. (This would be repeated many times in the future.) A crushing force came down on my body such that I could not move and I was struggling to breathe. There was a presence in the room that was unmistakably evil. I had learned to speak the name of Jesus and was trying to get it out resulting in spit drooling down my chin. My wife heard me, threw her hand on my head and cried out to Jesus. The power broke and moved off of me immediately. It was so dark I couldn't see my hand in front of my face. My wife said, "Did you see it?" I said, "See what? I can barely see you." She pointed up to a corner of the ceiling in the room and said, "It was right there." I said, "What?" She said, "A hole that was blacker than the blackness of this room. There were things moving in and out of it." Later I would find after some investigation that the teenager who had previously lived there occupied that room and he had been heavily into playing Dungeons and Dragons with Ouija boards and other fun toys. He had unknowingly opened a window into hell. No wonder it took two of us. The bible says one can set a thousand to flight and two can handle ten thousand (Deuteronomy 32:30). I couldn't do it without my wife. We had encountered a host from hell. Thank God for a spirit filled soul mate! No wonder my son was always afraid to go in there. Our prayer warriors returned and showed us how to close the opening. We were taught to use our authority. We were never bothered again.

We were at the point of changing churches and many others had already left for one reason or another. Perhaps what I was receiving was in fact a word of correction for this leadership and they refused to hear it from this novice lamb of no reputation and the success they had known was dwindling away. I don't know. I'm not the judge, but my wife made it clear that we needed to find another place. It wasn't supposed to be this way.

We never got the chance to change. During this time the Lord moved on us to go back to school. There was a college in Louisiana and we both wanted to be trained for ministry. She had been called since she was fourteen years of age, too, but had told the Lord she would

the "I wish I had listened to you" look. Finally, it was over. Aaron sat up, hopped off the table and went off to collect his presents. I fainted. When he came back with balloon and gift in hand I was on the table with blood pressure gear, wet towels, etc., in place. He looked at me and said, "What are you doing, Dad? It's time to go home." We had moved into the window where I no longer had insurance or a job. I related this to the doctor at one point, regarding our situation, once we reached Louisiana. "Send me a bag of beans so I can make red beans and rice and we'll call it even," he said. Thank you, Lord!

Now we rejoiced together as we moved ourselves into the position we felt God was directing us to take in an effort to become more knowledgeable of Him in a Christian ministry training facility. We went forward with great joy not knowing how we would pay for anything but happy to be in God's will....and I held her hand.

Chapter 6

A SPIRITUAL COURSE

The move to the duplex that would be our new home was complete. I was able to find a job at a wholesale parts house pulling parts down near the river. Our income level was certainly taking a downturn but we had adjusted our expenses to accommodate the change. We went through the admissions process for the bible college and signed up for two classes each. There was an excitement to be back in a college setting and there were a lot of older folks just like us thirtyish students. It seemed there was a real hunger to know more of God in everyone we encountered which made the experience all the richer.

Probably the most significant event in the teaching process occurred early in one of my wife's classes. It was an event that would forever change her thinking. I remember the day she came home from that class and how upset she was....not at the instructor, but in how she had been instructed all of her life. She felt absolutely betrayed.

The class had started that day with the instructor asking everyone to take the time to write down the Ten Commandments. He wanted to know if everyone really knew what they were. My wife dutifully wrote them out as she knew them quite well. This was not a problem for her at all. She was shocked when the instructor checked the work in class and she was told she had not gotten them correct. She declared that this was not possible. She had been reciting and reading them for many years. The instructor opened his bible and showed her Exodus 20. For the second commandment she had written, "Thou shalt not take the name of the Lord thy God in vain." She read the actual commandment as it is correctly stated in the King James (and some other translations) which said, "Thou shalt not make unto thee any graven image, or any likeness of anything that is in heaven above, or that is in the earth beneath, or that is in the water under the earth: Thou shalt not bow down thyself to them, nor serve them (pray to them)......". The whole lifelong practice of praying to statues was shot down by the truth. The church we were in had determined during the "dark ages" to rewrite God's commandments to try to win back people who had gotten into the occult practices that often drew the Israelites away to false worship. They eliminated the one that was a problem for them and divided another one in two to get back to ten. Of course, the scripture that says we are all saints was stretched to lift some folks to a higher level of "saint" which is also contrary to God's law to justify making "good" statues thereby ensuring contact with God through this source. When Jesus died He declared we had direct access to God and could approach Him ourselves through His shed blood and ask what we would in His (Jesus) name. That meant His name only. Asking in anyone else's name denies Christ's work on the cross and is an unheard prayer with no hope of answer from God. Those that get answered are answered by Satan. "Oh, come on now! Satan answering prayers! He can't do that!" Please reference Matthew 4:8-10. Satan offers Jesus anything in the world that He wants if He will just bow His knee and worship Satan. He had, and has, the power to give anything. When you bow a knee before any image, whether it depicts good or bad, you are bowing a knee before Satan. You are in direct violation of the true second commandment. And Satan will answer to keep you deceived and in error. He's after your soul and deception is his favorite weapon. (Even the most elect will be deceived if Jesus doesn't come soon.) The Spirit of God had opened our eyes to the deception and it changed everything. The walls of deception and religion began to crash down.

There would be more to come that would be tied to the call that had come on my life years ago when I was fourteen. Twenty-four years had transpired and we were about to enter a walk that would last twenty-four months. My family was going to endure hardship such as we had never known while at the same time God would use us mightily through many of His gifts of the Spirit as they would from time to time find fruition in these vessels that were being remade.

I will never understand why God does things the way He does or picks whom He sometimes picks. Surely He does not pick and choose as the world does. Often times it is the helpless, hapless lamb or the least among the brethren that receives a mission that only God can fulfill. Perhaps it is that way because the chosen one is completely dependent on God to accomplish the assignment thus being open to direction. One of the gifts I had flowing in me was the gift of knowledge with accompanying gift of exhortation, encouragement and correction (some call it the gift of prophecy....I call it the messenger, or watchman, service). I won't go into detail, but after one semester of college we were unable to continue due to finances and just involved ourselves in other ministry opportunities available there to learn as much as we could. We were avid attenders of every church service, classes through the church and every special function with all of the associated guest preachers. The bounty was huge as we sat under the teaching of not only the head of the institution, but many other Spirit filled guests who frequented the meetings. We read our bibles voraciously and absorbed the teachings. We were growing by leaps and bounds. The constant presence and flow of God's Holy Spirit was something we had never experienced before and we grew immensely just being in that flow.

All was not perfect, however, as nothing that man has an involvement in ever is no matter how hard we try. We all have weaknesses that the devil likes to probe to bring us down. As stated previously, I had mine, too. My failures, repentance and restoration had made me quite compassionate as I once said for those who fought similar battles. You just never think that those who have risen to the top have any such problems. If you think I'm about to go into detail, you are absolutely wrong. I don't need to add to what has already been written. If you want a good in depth analysis of what went on for a number of years you can pick up a book entitled, "Jimmy Swaggart: The Anointed Cherub that Covereth" written by Patricia Sunday. I'm going to stick with what God was doing in me and my wife as we walked through this space of time.

My first shake up came one day when I was sitting in church listening to a sermon. Suddenly my thoughts were infiltrated by things that were greatly troubling to me. I was terribly upset by what I was thinking (the devil works on the mind to steal the heart) especially since I was sitting in church. Before I go further I must explain that this was prefaced by a very vivid dream that took place in an old neighbor's house from the days when I was a child. This ironically was the home where my problems started. I entered the door of the home which entered into the kitchen area and was startled to hear someone off to the side screaming, "My, God! My, God! Look what someone has done!" I leaned across the table which always sat in the middle of the room to see a small baby lying on the floor. The legs of the child were tucked up next to its head with its arms over the back of the ankles pinning them down. The child was in the form of a cross on the floor. The hands had two huge nails driven through them and the child appeared as though dead. I screamed in horror at what I was seeing and grabbed the table and chairs in front of me throwing them out of the way as I struggled to get to the child. Once in front of the child I reached down and grabbed the nails to pull them out. As I grabbed the nails they turned into thorns and I pulled them out of the hands. I slipped my hands under the armpits of the child and began to lift him up. As I did so color came into his face and blood began gushing from the hand wounds. As I pulled the child to myself the blood began flowing over my shirt and down my back and I could feel myself being soaked. A voice spoke from the side and said, "You are getting blood all over you." I shouted, "I don't care! I don't care!" I was weeping uncontrollably. The voice spoke again and said, "You are covered in the blood." I woke up.

Some told me this child represented the preacher whose church I was in as events would transpire. It's possible. I think it also represented me as this was the house where my sin had found increase from other bad beginnings and would go from here to other places where it would be a thorn in my flesh. My repentance had put this to rest, but the dream was to prepare me for properly handling what God was about to reveal to me. Please understand that when God uses the gift of knowledge in you it is not given so you can use your knowledge to destroy another soul. (God does not desire that any should perish.) What is done in secret God will expose in due time. Your job is to pray for the soul that is in trouble and move for their restoration when the sin finds the light of day. God was about to separate a lot of goats and sheep.

Now back to the ugly thoughts penetrating my mind in the middle of church services. I was so upset I went down to the altar and I was weeping before the Lord asking Him how this could possibly be going on in my head. Surely I was the lowest form of life on earth. I was miserable. I thought this sort of thing was behind me. Suddenly I had a violent shaking hit me and I felt my head being forced upward to come face to face with the preacher who happened to be standing in front of me. I had revealed to me (not in intimate detail, but the area of the problem he was battling) that which the whole world would know about in approximately six more weeks. I was in total shock. I was as guilty as anyone else having lifted this man up to a place where I thought he was invincible and needed nothing. This was the man God had told me to watch "as he had words He would have me hear...." I literally stumbled away from the altar around the back of a section and took a post on an up ramp over at the side and stood looking back at this man. Suddenly I began to weep openly and I could not turn my gaze away. I was filled with absolute compassion for I knew what the revelation of this would bring. Once again, it was my job to pray for him and not destroy him. He belonged to the Lord. The Lord would bring the humbling in His time. The preacher turned toward me as he was singing, saw my countenance, dropped the microphone to his side and began to weep. He knew that I knew. His wife looked around from the other side of Him and directly at me and began to wring her hands. In that moment I realized that she apparently knew also. That would be the beginning of all efforts to isolate me from the preacher though I had many things the Lord would give me after the revelation of the sin became public.

And don't get the idea that God used me to pummel him. It was quite the opposite. His repentance was real. He was totally humbled and I heard him many times only a few feet from me crying out to God for this black cloud to lift off of his life, asking Him to forgive him for all of the pain he had caused to others, but more, for the damage this had done to God's kingdom. God would use the events to clean up His house. The people were about to have their measure taken. Those that were there in flesh pursing the flesh man left in an embittered angry mass. The ones who stayed understood God's mercy and the command we were given to "restore such a one as this". Those who won't forgive will receive judgment according to that which they have meted out.

A call to intercession had taken place on that up ramp. Suddenly I knew why I was here. This man had caused a tremendous spiritual growth in me by challenging everything I thought I knew and holding it up against the truth of God's word. There were others I would find who were called to this, but my focus became discovering each day what God wanted done in the area of interceding for this man. All of my efforts would be prefaced by two dreams. The first one I did not understand until the events described above took place. The realization of this revelation caused me to question God as to how I could possibly be of any assistance as I had my own weaknesses and struggles. The first dream was of me walking into the middle of a football field at about the 50 yard line. On one end was a lone individual and on the other end I caught my first glimpse of the hordes of hell. Hollywood can't duplicate the evil or the insidious faces I looked into, but they come close. I took my stand to protect the lone man on the other end as the hordes advanced. I was puffed up and ready to fight. They weren't getting past me! I was mowed over like I wasn't even there. A depiction I suppose of where I was with spiritual power.

I asked God what I was to do and as events transpired for the world to see I felt compassion rise up within me. I was not going to stomp on the fingers of a man who was on his face trying to get up. My wife and I joined in this charge from God and began to pray as we were led of the Spirit. During these months of the ministry being assaulted on every side from without the cry from within me placed there by God was "GET UP!" When repentance is real, restoration is immediate. The mess may take a while to clean up. The individual may still have battles ahead. The position and calling established by God are without repentance. One is reinstated and told to go forward. The spiritual growth during this time for me personally as this battle raged is something I can't find the words to explain. I asked God at one point where I was with Him. The dream recurred. Again I stood in the middle of a football field in the same situation. This time I saw myself walking towards the hordes of hell, but I was not the same man. I was not puffed up. I was simply confident in who was in me and what was being released in my inner most being. A mist rose over the field and I strode forward into the midst of the enemy forces. I remember that these hideous creatures began to recoil and withdraw from me in fear. The Spirit of God was showing me that He was my strength in the midst of my weakness. The blood had set me free, the Spirit had entered in and the power source was fully tapped because of it. It was resident within me and no power on earth could stand against it. I had to choose on every occasion to tap that source in the future. When I did not I fell to defeat. When I did the victory was assured.

It was much easier to find a seat from then on and my wife and I had no question in our minds but that we would stay. The words that God gave me were words of exhortation to get up and encouragement to go forward in the calling given to the preacher. I was able at first to hand them to him, but soon I was cut off by guards and other sentries whose charge I would find was to keep me away. I would then give the hand written messages to whoever God told me to give them to. I always assumed the words would get in and did hear responses from the pulpit that would indicate that was the case. Whether that was because the actual message was received and read or, as the Holy Spirit showed me, that when His word went in it had effect whether the primary person read it or not, I do not know. The Spirit of the word was released into that place.

Since the initial words were positive I was called a prophet. I never made any such claim. Time went on and fear began to grip the place for some unknown reason. What had been the most powerful move of the Holy Spirit we had ever encountered flowed in this place at every service. The ones who remained loved the Lord and had administered forgiveness and unconditional acceptance of this fallen man. The truth is he had not fallen from God's grace but had fallen into God's grace. This was something the world could not understand. It is a privilege that those of us who love the Lord are entitled to in the event we fall to the temptations of sin. Those that can't forgive don't get forgiveness. Those who try to exact the full measure will have the full measure exacted from them one day down the road. My wife and I chose to give what we had received.

Yet, I remember so distinctly the tests that God had in place for us. There was a day when I was in a hurry to leave and I stood to move up the aisle. My gaze fell upon a "tramp" seated in the front row of a section with hat in hands. He looked like he was right out of a Norman Rockwell cartoon. The look on his face was drawing me to him. Oh, but I didn't have time. I had to go. I walked past him, smiled and kept on trucking. For three weeks it seemed as though the heavens were brass when I prayed. I finally went before the Lord at a Saturday night prayer service and asked what I had done. I had a vision of this man sitting on that pew. I heard the Lord say "I visited you and you received me not." It wouldn't happen again. It didn't matter that everyone walked past him. I did. And the Spirit had quickened me to act.

There also came another day of great testing. We sat at home one evening wondering where our oldest son was, who was going to be in a lot of trouble when he showed up as he was disobeying me by running with some boys who were leading him in the wrong direction. I suddenly felt a strong warning in my spirit. I jumped up from the table and looked at my wife telling her I needed to go get Aaron. Something was wrong. I ran out the front door and headed down the block in the direction of the busy roadway near us only to encounter two of the boys Aaron wasn't allowed to be with coming towards me. At the same time I began to hear sirens. They shouted, "Aaron was just run over by a car." The enemy was trying again! I ran all the harder and came around the corner at the roadway to see a crowd gathered in the middle of the road. I froze momentarily and clutched my knees with my hands trying to get my composure crying, "Oh, God, no!" I quickly ran to the group of people and pushed my way through not knowing what I would see. My son sat being tended to by emergency technicians but he was conscious. I sat down on the road next to him and took him in my arms. His leg had been passed over by the car and you could see the tire mark indentations in his leg. The bone in his upper leg had come through puncturing a hole. Thankfully, no main vessels had been involved. I sat right there in the road and prayed out loud to God. By this time my wife had joined me and she prayed with me. As they loaded my son into the ambulance the driver of the car that struck our son told me he had caught site of Aaron in the last moment, had pulled the wheel and missed hitting him directly. Aaron had run into the side of the car and would have been unharmed if the tire had not passed over his leg.

I jumped in the ambulance with my son and shouted back to my wife where the ambulance was going. She ran back home with the other two boys, got the car and followed to the hospital. Aaron again had the privilege of having the doctor on duty that we were told took care of the LSU football players whenever they had serious injuries. He was top notch. Our son came out of surgery fully pinned to hold his bones in place and was put in harnesses in his bed. This was to be his state for three or four weeks according to the doctor until the bone had begun to join enough to go to a body cast.

To shorten the story I will simply say that a lot prayer went up and a lot of healing came down. My son was ordered not to get up and move around for several weeks. It took quite a while to get him out of the hospital as he was in traction and the first attempt at the body cast was unsuccessful. Once in it he was released to go home. After only a month at home my son came walking down the hallway Frankenstein style in his body cast. Up to that time we had been using a wheel chair that had been given to us to get him from place to place. I kept telling him to obey the doctor's orders. He kept insisting that God had healed him during one trip down to the altar at the ministry. We took him back to the doctor for his three month check- up and the doctor was extremely upset with him that the foot was walked off of the cast on the one side and the holding post in the middle was loose. He got after me for allowing him to get up and walk. I indicated I tried but I couldn't watch him every minute. The doctor then decided to take some x-rays to see if he had done any damage to the bone that needed to join itself back together.

The nurse brought the x-rays back in after a time and he stood looking at them. He said, "Well, I guess we just as well go ahead and take this cast off. Your leg appears to be healed." The nurse stopped him and requested that he look at the charts again. This cast had only been on three months and he was supposed to be in it for a minimum of six months. The doctor looked at me and said, "He can't be healed. Something is not right here. We'll fix the foot on the cast and come back in 30 days and we'll look again." So they did.

During the next month the cast began to deteriorate again as Aaron continued to walk around. I was putting it back together with duct tape. I said, "Lord, Aaron says you healed him and the doctor confirmed it with the x-rays. If this cast is no longer needed then cause it to disintegrate." Within the week the post in the center broke loose, the foot portion of the cast came apart and the body portion cracked down the middle. I said, "That's it. It's coming off." I grabbed a set of channel locks and busted the cast off a piece at a time. Once off Aaron got up and has been walking since that day with no residual problems. You should have seen the look on the doctor's face when Aaron walked in for his next appointment in street clothes and tennis shoes.

Now back to the churches battles. So what had brought about this fear in the church? I did not get any knowledge on this but suddenly realized that people were once again leaving. Whatever the reason many of them seemed to encounter me at one point or another and express what was happening to them. I did not seek them out. I was kept blind to what was transpiring this time. What was clear to me was that whether they declared themselves innocent or guilty of some purported sin, they were receiving no mercy and were summarily asked to vacate the premises. It was rampant.

The words that I then began to receive were words of correction. Long story, short (read the other book) I was now called a false prophet because the messages were not pleasing. I furthered my demise by inadvertently seating myself next to the widow lady who had taken me and my family in while she was sitting next to someone who had been labeled as a heretic and worse. I didn't even know who this person was. But as we were introduced I gave a Godly Christian embrace. I turned back toward the pulpit to a barrage of horrified looks. I had been counted among the transgressors I would find out.

This time we would become acquainted with a small group of people who regularly gathered and prayed for the man and the ministry. Though declared a heretic, the woman we had met was zealous about keeping the focus on prayer and would not tolerate any negative conversation or gossip entering. We would also find eventually that the woman of the house where we met had been called by God to walk out a spiritual birth which had some manifestations in the physical body. Her body went through changes but the time for normal delivery had passed. The ministry now declared her to be a problem. Our whole group was marked. The great irony was that no matter how God allowed us to look on the outside every member was a fervent advocate for the ministry and the man. We had some great intercessory prayer.

Let me extract a bit of my wife's writing on this. I will give what covers this incident and fill in the rest of her writings later in the book when it pertains to the proper time frame. My wife wrote: "This lady was a student at the Bible College. The normal time for delivery had passed. I placed my hand on her small belly and it was hard and there was life there. Some of us did not understand what was going on. An ultimatum was given to this woman by the pastor to deny her pregnancy or her children would be removed from the academy at the ministry. She gave in. Her husband became very disillusioned by the entire event and the family would eventually leave the ministry a year later."

"In the aftermath, I had shared with them the promise that God had given to us. He had asked me on the way home from the previous meeting at the house of this couple if I would take up where this lady had left off. I said, "Yes, Lord." I had the promise of a double portion given to me for my obedience. God gave my husband names. She felt led to give me all of her maternity clothes and did so. I became pregnant three months later. I went through a strong hormonal change and became achy, crabby and felt sick to my stomach right away. The Lord told me that I was pregnant around the end of May, 1990." End of quote.

Future events would see me forbidden to come to the altar to pray for anyone, as well as being asked on three different occasions not to come back. I had to obey the Lord, however, and on future return visits the message that I was unwelcome would be restated. Finally I walked to the back of the church under the leading of the Holy Spirit and shook the dust off of my shoes.

My wife stood with me throughout this time as an encourager and also a confirmer. We would always be on the same wave length on these spiritual matters. It was more than one could ask to have a soul mate who also flowed with the Spirit confirming our direction. She had to be strong because even as the Lord used me to do these things, we began to go through the "recompense of my reward" for having walked away from the Lord. We moved to a small house just in time for me to lose my job. Try as I might I could not get a job anywhere. It was becoming desperate. I took yard jobs but would get poison ivy so bad we had to spend the money to get rid of it. I was deathly allergic and it was quite prevalent in the area. I stood in lines to get boxes of food. I was humbled beyond measure. My wife took a job at a popular breakfast restaurant and I stayed home with three small boys. This would go on for months. She barely made enough at $2.50 per hour plus tips to pay the rent and utilities, but we made it and had a whole $25.00 a week left over for groceries. We lost a good bit of weight.

One night we came up a little short on food and I cooked up the last of the macaroni and cheese to feed the boys. My wife and I would drink a glass of water before meals so we could feel full after we ate. That night my middle son came up and said, "Daddy, I'm still hungry." I had nothing to give him. I walked into the bedroom, shut the door and wept before God. He said, "Many of my children go to bed hungry every night." This comment would initiate a concerted effort on our part to go to Honduras. I would even speak to the daughter of a man running for President as we also were trying to adopt two boys from there. I had a chance to witness to her, but none of our other determined efforts bore any further fruit.

What the Lord did say to me in that bedroom was, "Take everything that you have and put it out on the driveway and I will provide." We had a sale the next day for which I only put up a sign over on the busy roadway near us. I told my wife what had happened and she declared that we must obey. She knew it was from the Lord. When I say we put everything out there, we put everything out there. As we sat out under the awning we would hear the Spirit tell us who was coming, what they would buy and how much to ask for it. I had never before had such an experience. It happened in each and every case just as He said.

At one point I looked at my wife and said, "Someone is coming to buy these 10-speed bikes." Within five minutes they drove up, looked at the bikes, returned to their car and began to drive away. We looked at each other. I said, "I guess that wasn't them." The car stopped in front of the neighbors and the man stood up in the door of his car and shouted, "Set those bikes back. I'm going to run over to the bank and get the money. We'll be right back." The bikes sold just like the Lord said. When they came back they stayed and really probed us as they could see our furniture and everything was out there. My wife opened up to the lady with the truth of our situation. They finally left.

We went to get groceries with the money that had come in so we could eat that night. I've never had a garage sale where everything sold, but that is exactly what happened. We had nothing left. One family even walked back up to us and gave us $50.00 just because the Lord told them to. My wife told me that she was sure the Lord had told her not to spend more than $70.00 and not to buy meat. Just buy enough for today and breakfast. We obeyed.

During the night I had a vivid dream indicating that someone was coming to the house and we needed to be there. When I awoke I petitioned the Lord about it as we had promised the boys we would take them over to the park that day. I hadn't even had money for gas so we hadn't been able to do even a little thing for them. I asked Him to please allow us to do this and have us back in time. It was clear to me that I was to write a note, draw a map of where we would be and ask these people from the dream to find us there. I did it and hung it on the front door. We drove away with our happy boys who got to go play at the park. No one ever showed up. As I drove back I assumed that what I thought was a real stretch, though I left the note, was probably just that. We pulled into the driveway and I noticed immediately that there was writing on the note. We retrieved the note and it said to go to the back patio and then to our neighbors across the street.

On the back patio we found sacks of groceries. It would last us a month or better. At the neighbors we found meat in the freezer....meat we hadn't been able to afford in months. And that meat lasted us longer than the other groceries. Something we found in one sack gave away who had been used to bless us. My wife picked up on it and had gotten the phone number of the buyers of the bikes so we could keep up with them. The lady answered and asked how my wife had known. They had tried to conceal their identity. She told my wife that she had a dream the night before and God had showed her that they were to do this for us. God required our obedience to sacrifice all that we had and provided exceedingly and abundantly more than we expected. We had enough money to pay the rent because we didn't have to buy food.

This was a temporary fix, however, as my walk was not yet complete and my family would continue to suffer through it. I had found a job in a burger place for a while but it ultimately closed down. That happened to three companies that hired me during this time. I didn't understand what was happening to me. I began to feel like Jonah, but I was obeying. Finally we got behind on the rent to where we were going to have to leave but had nowhere to go. Mind you that the stress of everything with the battles at that church and our financial woes multiplying was testing my faith to the limit. Honestly, I was beginning to fail and turn back to my sinful ways. Don't misunderstand what I am saying....I was never unfaithful to my wife though the devil tried dangling that carrot often. God's grace was sufficient. The rest you don't need to know about. It was just ugly. And my repentance would be required again. Yet, God used these occasions to make me stronger each time I admitted my weakness and need for him to take this burden from me. "Please, Lord. Take this thorn from my flesh!" Each time his answer was "My grace is sufficient for you." My compassion for others was finding an increase.

As we were about to be out on the street, my wife determined to go to a prayer meeting she was invited to and ask for prayer for our situation. While she shared our dilemma expressing God's promise that He would provide, a little old widow lady (the one who got me in trouble because of where she was sitting when I sat next to her—reference a few paragraphs back) declared that this was not going to be. We were going to come and live with her in the little one bedroom apartment she had just rented when she came from California. How she got there I do not know. She showed up with her clothes in the car and a bookcase sticking out of the trunk of her little Datsun, a car that appeared to burn more oil than gas. It had to be God that she even survived the trip. We were about to be put up with a widow lady for six months that God had sent to rescue us in our hour of need. We shouldn't have even been able to stay with her. It was against the rules but the managers looked the other way. There were many in our complex that did take the time to deride us severely for taking advantage of this poor old widow lady with the huge cancerous growth on her face. We didn't have to defend ourselves. She would march right out and set the folks straight on her own. You didn't mess with her. We stayed until God provided me another job and we got our own apartment.

We did take a sojourn to our home stomping grounds in Nebraska about this time as my brother was getting married and he wanted me to speak at his wedding. We had gathered a little money from the new job and they cleared me to go. (It was here that the invitation to Colorado would become formal from another brother and my sister to help them in their new business.) Once there I found time at last to go outside to seek the Lord about what He would have me say at this wedding. It was while walking the walk outside my parent's home that I asked the Lord why everything had been so hard when I was doing my best to obey His every command. I received an immediate response and dashed inside to speak to my mother. I asked her when it was that I told her that I heard the Lord call me into his service. She looked surprised expressing the thought that she had expected that was long lost from my memory. She said, as I have stated earlier because of this event, "You were 14. Why do you ask?" I looked at my wife who was sitting there and I said," I was told there had been one month for every year that had passed since the day God had called me until now. During that time He had taken away everything that I had earned on my own including my ability to use my education to obtain work. I had strayed for twenty four years and twenty four months had now passed. That season was over and He would provide from this day forth according to His plan for my life." I was given a rather dynamic message for my brother's wedding. A few were offended but he and most others received it. I speak what I am given to speak.

Our next phase awaited us when we returned to Louisiana. The new job I had would once again be short lived as the company was sold out and they released all employees except for one truck driver....and that wasn't me. I couldn't believe it, but the contact I had already with my brother and sister regarding their business in Colorado would now bear fruit. This job in Louisiana ran out at the same time as our apartment lease. I was worn out. I couldn't stay in the battle anymore despite knowing the twenty four month ordeal was declared to be over. I can't honestly tell you if I disobeyed God in this or not, but we did pray and we both felt we were released to go to Colorado. I packed what little we had in a small trailer, hooked it up behind our Nova and off we went. We nearly got killed on Raton Pass as the car faltered going up the mountain and began to roll backwards. An 18-wheeler was barreling up the road behind us and didn't slow up a bit. I thought, "What is this guy doing? Can't he see I'm in trouble and rolling back?" I fought the wheel and the car died making things worse. It was overheating. I struggled to fire the engine and had no success, continuing to fight the brake and steer a trailer laden car out of the way. My wife shouted, "Jesus! Jesus! Jesus!" Suddenly my attempts at steering, which had been unsuccessful, cooperated and I can only say a huge hand also took that car and trailer placing it perfectly on the service portion of the road when I had it partially jack-knifed. This all happened in a matter of seconds. We really didn't have time to think. The moment we slid on to the service area the 18-wheeler roared by never having slowed up for even a moment. We would have half a dozen events with overheating as we went up through Eisenhower Tunnel which problems were finally resolved by a man stopping, removing my thermostat core and telling us to replace it when we got where we were going. We shouldn't have any more trouble. We didn't. I will say that each and every time we overheated we came to a convenient stop right near one of the water barrels located here and there along the way. Ours was a common problem.

Colorado. Who would have thought…? Well, here we were, somewhat the worse for wear but ready to find out what God had in store for us. My wife sat next to me at the end of the harrowing part of our journey and we took in the beauty of the mountains and streams. It made you feel closer to God….and I held her hand.

Chapter 7

ELIJAH'S BROOK

I did not title this chapter in this manner to make any sort of declaration about myself, but it simply felt during the year that we would spend here that I had unfinished business where we had been. My escape from the spiritual wars would be allowed for a season, but a return date had been emblazoned on the horizon whether it was to my liking or not.

We began to settle into this area in Colorado that was surrounded by mountains on three sides and slipped out into the desert on the west. It had its own beauty in all four areas and we explored and enjoyed them to the fullest....particularly the Grand Mesa which rose to 10 or 11,000 feet harboring a beautiful stream, woods and meadows. The air up there was so refreshing. We felt exhilarated and renewed each time we visited.

Our adventure started with a move to my sister's home with her family. I was struggling with the move and all of the aforementioned trials. I was lacking in patience with our surroundings and the differing philosophies of life between our two families. They were fun to be around but each family needs its own space to accommodate their own lifestyles. Once I was working for them and a little money came our way we began to investigate apartments that we could rent. Prices were high in the valley but we finally found a place we could handle with the income level I would have and moved in. This new location would bring a myriad of experiences.

There was a neighbor a few doors down whose brother took up residence and began to draw the young kids of the area. He started out on reasonably good footing but he had a past and still struggled with it. It wasn't long before he was back in the party mode and I had concerns about possible drug use. I did talk with him and share about the Lord but he wasn't in a place where he was desirous of real change. I made it clear to my sons that his place was off limits which irritated both him and them. He did his best after that to be as contrary as he could primarily by using an obnoxious noise factor. One day when he was outside blasting his speakers I walked out my front door in full view of him and his friends, raised my hands to the sky, lifted my voice and shouted, "Lord, if this young man is using this stereo system as a weapon against me then it shall not stand! Take it away from him right now!" Almost immediately the sound stopped and I saw him looking over his speakers and looking over at me. We never had another problem. Unfortunately I later heard he was picked up on drug charges and returned to jail for a rather long stay.

We had another neighbor across the street who exhibited irrational behavior on a regular basis. You would often see him outside walking in circles talking to someone who wasn't there. We stayed clear as I was sure I knew what the problem was but had no leading to deal with it. One day I heard a large commotion outside and looked out to see another neighbor in a confrontation with this man. Realizing the potential danger that my other neighbor was in I walked out and asked him to come away for a moment from the verbal exchange. I quickly tried to explain what he was up against and the power that was contained there. He looked at me rather strangely. At that point I felt a presence next to me and turned to see the other gentleman with rage in his eyes. I spoke to him and told him he needed to go back inside his apartment. He was drooling spittle on his chin and slurring vehement words at me as he raised his arm and fist to strike me. I grabbed him in a bear hug pinning his arms against his sides and stood with his nose right on mine. The other neighbor was hollering, "Hit him! Hit him!" to which I responded, "That is not what he needs." I looked directly into the eyes of this man and I saw the demon dancing in his eyes. I shouted, "In the name of Jesus Christ I command you to loose this man and come out of him!" By now a crowd had gathered that had taken up the fight chant but my words silenced them. The man in my arms began to slump against me and his eyes rolled back leaving only the whites to look at. He continued to drool with something unintelligible coming from his mouth. Again I shouted, "I have authority over you. I told you in Jesus name to come out and you have to leave!" People started backing away as the man slumped further in my arms at which time a sheriff showed up, threw open the door of his car and pointed his weapon in our direction commanding me to let go of the man I was holding. I replied that I did not think he could stand up on his own. He ordered me again to do what he said and I let go. The man got his footing and backed quickly away from me.

After all of the interviews had taken place I was still ticketed for "disturbing the peace" along with both neighbors who had been involved. The sheriff said he didn't really want to give me a ticket at all having heard the testimony of what went on but he had no choice. We all had a court date in our future.

At the court hearing I was totally naïve as to the process having never been in this situation before so God used the neighbor that I had gone out to rescue to enlighten me. He told me I would be called up and I was to appeal to the Assistant District Attorney as I recall. At any rate, he said, "Don't plead guilty. This will give you a chance to plead your case." I did as I was instructed following right in behind my neighbor which then found us assigned to a hallway to await our opportunity to make our statement. My neighbor was pacing up and down between the rows of people on either side of the hallway, shaking his head, waving his hands and worried that things were going to go badly for him. He unfortunately knew his way around this place. After a while I calmly confronted him and said so that everyone could hear, "God sent me out to help you the day this all happened. He is not going to forsake me or you in this situation. You need to settle down and watch what God is about to do. This will not stand."

Shortly thereafter we were called into a room containing a long table with people seated at the other end. We were told to seat ourselves to one side and waited as a man at the end of the table shuffled through some papers. The other neighbor had not shown up. Another door opened just as my neighbor had been told to state his case and a gentleman walked to the end of the table. He had a brief discussion with the gentleman with the briefcase which he then closed. They both looked at us for a moment. The gentleman with the briefcase stood up and said, "You are free to go. All charges against you have been dropped." We hadn't spoken a word. My neighbor went down the hallway outside and gave the testimony to those who had heard me encourage him earlier. "He was right! He was right! We didn't have to say a word! All the charges were dropped!"

Sometime later I would see the "no show" neighbor outside with people whom I took to be his parents. I was walking in front of my apartment and he pointed at me directing the attention of the people with him towards me. He was calm and exhibited none of the agitation that was always present in him before. They looked at me but never spoke and went inside. We never saw this man exhibit any of these tendencies again. Shortly thereafter he moved away.

The following year from the business standpoint would involve grueling hours as any new business start- up requires. All of us put in a lot of hours and the children spent a lot of playtime in the back of the shop after school as well as on the weekends while the adults worked. We escaped as often as we could.

After our initial move to our own place we drove around looking for a church. As we drove down a local highway we passed by an old church that was bustling with activity. I glanced at it briefly and the driver continued on. Suddenly I received one of those "spiritual" attention grabbers. I found myself whirling around, looking out the back window and saying to my wife, "We are supposed to go to this church." She said, "Let's go check it out."

We arrived at the front door a little later as we could not stop at the time. I found the pastor and greeted him. I began asking him about his church which was an early 1900's relic. They were still remodeling but they were having services. He asked where we were from. I told him. His eyes got really big and he began to ask all sorts of questions about me personally. He really dug deep. I made it clear to him that while we had been active at the ministry mentioned we were not part of the ministry. We had just been there and participated in volunteer ministries over time. Well, he had been writing that ministry and contacting them requesting that someone would be sent out to help him establish his church. He had gotten no response. Again I told him that I was not who he was assuming I was. I just happened to be there because of the business venture my family had begun. He was happy regardless. Like it or not we were God's answer to his prayers. He invited us back to church on Sunday making sure we planned to attend Sunday school classes.

We walked up the steps on Sunday and the pastor stood smiling broadly at the door. He handed me the book for the Sunday school lesson and I joked that I would try not to go to sleep while he taught. He said, "I'm not teaching. You are." I was dumbfounded. No preparation and no warning. I started to protest but he would not be dissuaded. I looked at my wife and she said, "You can handle it. Just read the text and go from there. The Holy Spirit will help you like He always does." He did. I taught that class during the time we were there occasionally ruffling some religious feathers with truths I had learned over the past few years of study and "sitting at the feet of the master (Jesus)". The Holy Spirit had taught me truth. I was then asked to lead worship as they had no musicians and no leader. Talk about a desperate situation, but my darling Princess had leaked it that I had done it before and that I had a reasonable voice. "Lord, I did not come here to be this busy," I protested. My wife and I began a long process of gathering songs, organizing them in groups and filing them for weekly selections. It was basically just the words as I have no ability to read music. I simply relied on having sung the songs before and sang in whatever key it was I sang in. It was successful, but by no means perfect.

The valley churches tried to have fellowship with one another which would result in us arriving back late to the church one evening to unload from the van and recover our own vehicles to go home. As we drove up I noticed a haggard man sitting on the curb in front of the church. It was me again, walking out of the church and seeing the tramp on the pew. I walked away from the group and knelt down in front of this man. I wasn't going to fail God again. As I spoke to him I studied his physical condition. He was shirtless and his jeans looked like he had been wearing them for a year without washing them. He had no shoes on. He appeared to be drunk or on drugs but actually spoke quite clearly. There were nodules of some sort hanging from his armpits. I asked what we could do to help him. I asked if he needed a ride somewhere. It was late, but I didn't care.

I began to speak to him about how Christ could help him change his life so he didn't have to live like he was. He locked his eyes on mine. I thought, "Here is one who is going to hear." He acknowledged all that I had to say and I asked him if he would like to pray to receive Christ as His savior. He replied that he would. Each time we got to the part where we acknowledge that we are sinners and need to be forgiven, he would stop. He absolutely would not repeat that phrase. I tried three times.

By then the pastor had gotten everyone on their way and joined me by the curb. I told him where we were and the pastor indicated to him that we would take him down to a house he knew of. Folks in his situation were taken in for the night so they wouldn't have to be on the street. He agreed to go with us and seated himself in the back seat of the pastor's car. We spoke quite a bit and were able to extract his name. He volunteered little else, however. The house the pastor had spoken of appeared over the hood of the car and we stopped. The pastor went to the door returning a short time later with the message that because it appeared our charge was drunk they would not take him in. He had to sober up first.

Our next option, which the pastor knew of from previous efforts like this, involved a downtown location adjacent to the hospital complex as I recall. I could not believe the number of people that were there being treated and processed when we pulled up. The place was packed at 2:00 a.m. in the morning. We were escorted with our charge to a table where we were seated and asked to wait. I spoke further with the shirtless gentleman and told him we would be back to check on him the next day. He made it clear that he knew we wouldn't show up. I affirmed that we would surprise him. We would be there. At that moment a nurse walked up and called our charge by name. I was a bit surprised that she knew him. She took one look at him, then at us. "Did you in any way touch the nodules hanging down under his armpits?" she asked. "Yes," I said. "I laid hands on him and prayed that he would be healed." She said, "Come with me right now. We'll take him from here." I looked back at him and he stared at me with a fixed gaze. I shouted back, "Trust me! We will be back."

We were ushered into an area of sinks and handed some scrubbing soap. The nurse said, "You have come in contact with a highly contagious disease that the nodules under that man's arms are potentially able to spread. Please scrub yourselves thoroughly and then you may go. Stop first at the check in station to give us all of the information you have." We did as we were told and dutifully provided the name of the man he had given us along with answering several questions as to how we came to be there, our relationship to him, etc.

Being very tired we left. I glanced over at the table but did not see the man any longer. After a good night's sleep I rejoined the pastor at the church and we headed off to find the man. Driving back to the location where we had delivered him we discussed the previous evening's events and wondered how things had turned out. We arrived and moved toward the check in station. There we requested information on what they had done with the man we left there. They could not find any record or paperwork that would indicate that the episode ever took place. We then asked if we could contact the nurse who took him when we arrived. They had no such nurse on staff. Being obviously baffled, the gentleman talking to us said that it was possible that he could have been taken over to the hospital if his situation was considered serious enough and the paperwork might have gone with him.

We thanked him and proceeded to the hospital. We went through the same process there with no one having any knowledge of the admission of anyone with the name we gave. We were sent upstairs to another area and repeated the story there. A nurse overheard our conversation and said, "Wait a minute. I remember that name. Let me check a file." At last, we thought. We're getting somewhere. The nurse walked up with a file and said, "Repeat his name for me again." We did. She said, "That man died of Leukemia in this hospital six months ago." We stood absolutely speechless. Had we been tested? Had we entertained an "angel" of God without being aware? I looked at my pastor and said, "No wonder he wouldn't say the part about being a sinner."

Life at the church hit a new high after the revelation of this story. We had moves of God's spirit that were such a blessing. We were located in a rough part of the little city we were in. There was a biker bar down the street and prostitution was a common situation. Moonies sold their wares on the corner across the street.

We had a prostitute walk in during one service, walk straight down to the altar, as praise and worship filled the air inside and outside the church, and she began to weep. It was hard to imagine that our worship was acapella, yet it drew this one in. There were no musicians to be had so it was not by doctrine, just by necessity. It didn't inhibit the Holy Spirit. People immediately gathered around her and began to minister to her. Eventually she was escorted to another room where people stayed with her and prayed throughout the service. Word would eventually come the next Sunday that she had been miraculously set free, repented of her sins and was saved by God's grace. What a marvelous victory! The Spirit of God had drawn her in and we could take no credit for it other than we were doing what was on our hearts as we lifted up His name. The ugly that existed in our little fellowship surfaced shortly thereafter....amazingly with some who had prayed with this woman... when the pastor put her in the little choir they had formed to sing specials. She was a prostitute and should not be allowed to be in this position. The pastor stood his ground. She was free of her past and had as much right as anyone else to get up and sing God's praise. The core group that had been to other churches in the valley and caused problems flexed its religious muscle. They would be further aggravated when the pastor began to ride his motorcycle down past the biker bar wearing his big sombrero which allowed him to make contact and begin to minister there. Eventually he would perform marriages for them and see some of them come to the Lord.

In this time period we had one of the "Moonies" walk into church during a service and we had the same scenario take place as with the prostitute. Long story short, he accepted salvation, was baptized and sent back to his home up in the Great Lakes area within three weeks after his family was contacted. While he was with us the bigger church with all of the "bells and whistles" came to him and wanted him to attend their church. There was nothing going on in our church according to them. Having just been freed from the bondage of the Moon culture he wasn't buying what they were selling. Their hopes of parading him around as "their success" were dashed. I never cease to be amazed at how "full of themselves" some professed "Christians" can be.

Finally, the wrath of the little group in our church became focused on me. They demanded that the pastor get rid of me. They didn't want my singing and they found my teaching to be an affront to what they believed. He refused again. They were the big givers and they flexed that muscle, but again he refused to compromise. I was confronted by them in a shouting situation one morning as I taught something that rubbed them the wrong way. I pointed out to them the location of what I was saying in the bible. That had no bearing. They didn't want to hear it. They demanded that I leave. I said, "I'll still be standing here and you will all be gone when this is over." Three weeks later they were off with their itching ears to oppress some other poor pastor....and they took their money with them.

It got pretty tough but the pastor forged ahead and started taking in some homeless people. This would eventually get him shut down as those that left filed a complaint with the "home church" that was supporting this evangelistic effort and they, and the city, combined efforts to take the church away. Prior to the shutdown the pastor found a piano player. She was one of many that came from time to time and declared they could do a better job than me in leading worship. They typically lasted a week to two weeks and it would come back to me. Each time I willingly stepped out of the way. This last piano player had a major struggle with her plans to lead and it, too, lasted about two weeks. I was trying to sing along with her piano playing but she often refused to play music I had selected. That was a problem as I always prayed and asked God what songs to use and what order to put them in. She was about to touch something she did not understand. I simply indicated that the song would be a part of the service and it was acceptable if she chose not to play at that time.

Unfortunately, she had obtained a key to the church so she could come in and practice. We arrived on our usual day to get the music together to find all of the work we had done missing from the files. The pastor called her and asked her if she had the music. She did. She wasn't returning it either because we were breaking the law having copies of the words and using them. Hello. We weren't selling them. What kind of reasoning was this? Truth was she wanted to be in full charge and resented me using songs she did not think were appropriate. Hello, again. Praise songs that worshipped God were inappropriate.

All the work was gone and we had to start over. We heard this woman was quite ill and bedridden shortly after this. My wife went to see her, despite her actions, to minister to her. I went along. While there we would find out that this woman had an issue of blood and the doctors could not figure out what was wrong. My wife suggested that her actions in taking the music from the church might have opened the door to her illness. She became incensed and we left. We never did hear how her situation turned out. We were sure as to why it had occurred. You don't touch what God is doing. You may draw back a leprous hand.

While all of this was occurring we also had the promise growing before us. Let me return to my wife's testimony now shown in quotes. "I felt life for the first time when we arrived in Colorado. I started putting on weight but never got very big. Time rolled around for me to deliver but I was very small. The due date was February 12th and on that day I began the full experience of contractions that had come with my other pregnancies. My body would not deliver."

"I had no idea what I was to go through. I walked in front of the people at church and they wondered why I wasn't delivering. Why didn't I go to the doctor? (Something the Lord would not allow.) One lady even told me her aunt had delivered a nine pound tumor. She was concerned. I went through a great deal of internal torment and went before the Lord continually concerning the pregnancy. He always reassured me and told me the babies were fine. He was taking care of me. There was no miscarriage. The families thought there was something seriously wrong with me."

The day finally came when the date emblazoned in our future for the return trip to the place from which I had determined we must flee arrived. My wife and I both knew it. The second catastrophe was about to hit there which we did not know, but the call to be an intercessor for the one who had now spent years trying to defeat his flesh with his flesh (if I pray hard enough, often enough, read my bible incessantly and place a circle of guards around me to protect me from my weakness I'll be ok) was unrepentant. I had to go back. I was not happy. Neither was my family. They thought we had lost our minds. They knew from our sharing what a rough time we had when we were there. How could we possibly consider going back? Members of both of our families collaborated and sent the chosen disciples to investigate our mental well-being with the charge to take our children to protect them if need be. They picked the wrong crew. Once there they heard our testimony and took our part, though they surely could not fully understand. They just knew we weren't crazy.

We packed our things into another trailer and my brother used his truck to pull it over the mountain. We still had to face Raton Pass but we stopped in a park to eat and I waited until a cooler part of the day to help our cause. We made it over, but as we got into Texas the car started rolling steam up under the dash. I knew the heater core had let go and, even though we weren't using any heat, we were losing all of our coolant to the floor board in the front seat. I was able to get us to a truck stop a short distance away. We pulled in and parked. My wife took the kids inside. I was standing there looking at my dilemma when I heard a voice behind me. I turned to see a man and a young boy standing there. Where they had come from I do not know as I had parked in a big open area away from everything. He asked what the problem was. I told him. He asked if I had tools. I responded in the affirmative. He said, "Just cut this hose loose here, take that connection away and reconnect this hose there. That way you will bypass the heater core so you can fix it later." I thought to myself that I should have known that. I turned to say thank you after a brief glance at what he suggested. There was no one there. I looked all around the open expanse where I had parked and there was no one walking away from the area. I was used to this now. I looked up and said, "I guess I am going to the right place. You are with me. Thank you."

My wife returned and I told her what happened. She began to praise God and rejoice at His helping hand. We filled the car back up with water after the fix and continued on our journey back to Louisiana. We both had a sigh on our hearts as we discussed how it had been before. We shared that we would surely not have a repeat of those events but regardless we would obey. She slid over close to me as we drove into Louisiana from Texas...and I held her hand.

Chapter 8
THE GOOD, THE BAD, THE UGLY

W e had no idea where we were going to live. We grabbed a paper and began to look through the rental sections for Baton Rouge. Nothing seemed to connect for us in the way of an apartment. We were reasonably certain we were looking for a house. Once again the Lord began to use that gifting He had given my wife. She pointed us to a specific area of town and our search intensified. We found a house that was in a hidden away development not far from a river called the Amite. We had a little money but not a lot. I looked at the place and I was sure we would not be able to afford it. It was a lovely brick home with three bedrooms. It was amazingly close in style and floor plan to the house we had left behind in Oklahoma so many years before. Perhaps God was going to give back. The lady was happy to give us a tour. She was also very inquisitive as to our situation seeing we had an old car and a U-Haul trailer still attached. My wife retired to the kitchen with her and gave a brief synopsis of our situation without giving away too much information. She did tell the lady of the house where we were staying, which was just down the road at a dismal little motel that was so dark inside even the interior lights didn't help much. The lady said she would discuss things with her husband when he came home and let us know.

We had worn out our first day back. I have to admit a certain amount of dread began to creep in as I recalled past experiences. I wondered what we were in for this time. I compared notes with my wife and she was having the same feelings. Yet, she declared, "I'm sure God led us to that house. He will make a way." God had been working through all of our experiences to bring us into one accord and one mind with each other as well as with Him. We were always on the same page once we communicated. We did the best thing we had been trained to do in all of these challenges that had come our way. We joined hands, looked up and said this will require your intervention. We need some help. Your will be done.

We did not know that God had answered our prayers before we could get the prayers made known to Him. There was a knock at the door of the motel room. I opened the door into the darkness to see the lady who had the house standing there in tears. God had touched her heart and she simply could not stand the thought of us staying in the motel room we were in. She and her husband were leaving on a trip to Costa Rica that week and would be gone for the better part of the rest of the month. She insisted that we move into their home and house sit for them while they were gone. We were in shock! I stood there at a loss for words, but my lovely wife jumped right in, hugged her neck and said as she often did, "Thank you, Jesus, for this wonderful woman you have sent to help us!"

The next day found us moving our few belongings into the house. I was amazed that they moved some of their things out indicating they had purchased a town home, as I recall, and they would probably move in there or with one of their children if it wasn't ready for them when they returned from their trip. She and her husband had talked further after she had left us the night before. We found they intended to make this our home. They left most of the furniture when they realized we didn't have any. We would pay no rent for the first month because we were watching it for them. That would give me time to find a job and get some income started. (God had said that He was going to be our provision after our last ordeal found its completion and He had established my pathway.) He had sent us away for a year, or allowed us that time, and had brought us back watching over us all the way. He was doing for us what we could not do in the natural. We celebrated and gave Him praise for what He was doing in the midst of us.

Finding a job was a bit more difficult but God led me to a temporary service agency and they found work for me right away. My first little task was a project to stamp thousands of papers with consecutive numbers for a lawsuit. It took me and others on the assignment weeks to get it done. No matter. It was a job. It ended and we hit a dry spell.

My brother called me from Colorado indicating that the new computer system was giving them trouble and the books were in a mess. Would I please come out and help? God was at work. He had some unfinished business with me as I was struggling with this work stoppage and there was a need for me to know more of Him. I arrived in Colorado and buried myself in the project being upset with the Lord for taking me back to Louisiana to go through another time of difficulty. I was forgetting the testimony of Him in the very house He put us in. The wake up was on the way concerning my faith. About the third day on the job we went out to eat after work. I ate something that gave me the first case of food poisoning I had ever had. It hit me in the night and I was deathly ill. I remember lying on the bathroom floor losing everything from every direction. I thought I was going to die.

The next morning all I could do was lay on the couch in a limp, washed out, totally decimated body. Everyone made sure I was comfortable and went on to work. I was glad that they lived in a ranch home away from other houses because once alone I unloaded on God. I was seething with anger over just about everything. I took him right down the line recounting events that had not gone so well and forgetting the positives that were interlaced in the fabric. I screamed at the ceiling for hours. Every frustration and disappointment came out. I wish I could say He intervened and set me straight right then, but life grew blacker and darker for the next three days.

On the sixth night I lay in one of the kids bedrooms in my brother's house trying to get some rest before my departure the next day. Suddenly I was awakened by a presence in the room. I was not afraid. I saw in the spirit a form at the end of the bed. I realized what was happening and I declared rather harshly that I no longer wanted Him in my life. I had meant what I said. "Leave me alone!" I heard a voice say quite gently, "You are like so many of my children. I asked you to take up your cross and follow me. You went your own way." I protested recounting the moves we had made, the situations where I had declared His word and been tormented for it, the financial loss I had suffered, the situation my wife was walking through and finally this obedience to go back to a place we did not want to go. Again He spoke, "You have taken up your cross and obeyed my direction, but along the way you have hung on it the traditions of men and your own efforts loading it to the point that it is wearing you down. I never asked you to carry your cross this whole time. You were going on a short walk with me. Your flesh was going to be crucified. I would lift you up in new life. All I wanted you to do was walk with me, talk with me, do what you saw me doing and say what you heard me saying. You have gone your own way and now the weight of your fleshly efforts has caused you to turn away from me." Then I felt myself being lifted from the bed and drawn up to the chest of the One who stood before me by powerful arms as though I was a baby. I wept uncontrollably. I was sobbing out loud. I repeated that I didn't have any more to give and He needed to leave me alone. The love that flowed through me broke down every resistance that I had. I still get goose bumps when I recall it. I began to let myself fall fully into those arms and I began to rest. I have never felt such a powerful love.

The next morning my brother sat at the breakfast table with me as he prepared to take me to the airport. "Did you notice something strange going on in the house last night?" he asked. "Yes," I said. "I did." I would tell him some years later. We arrived at the airport and I got on the plane in the midst of a slight icing problem. The plane was one of those flying culverts and you had to stoop down to get to your seat. It was packed with people headed for Denver. I took out my bible and began to read as they declared we would be powered down for a deicing treatment. I felt led to go to First John 1:1-10 and read. As I read the Spirit came on me with tremendous convicting power and I began to fall apart. Thank God in that moment the lights were turned out and I faced the window next to me as I softly wept and asked God to forgive me of my sins. I went home a changed man with a new revelation of who this one I called Lord was. I had found intimacy beyond any effort I had ever engaged in and I had discovered a love that truly permeated every aspect of my being. I was physical, emotional (soul) and spirit. Those three things had to be completely under His control to know and receive His fullness. I was simply not fully submitted up to this time. I would share all of this with my wife when I got home. God also showed me that all three of these areas being submitted to Him would allow me to have the fullness I was missing with my wife, though I thought we were already one in the Lord. She had found that submission before me. Every aspect of our relationship grew deeper and stronger from this time. I didn't know that more was possible. My Princess rejoiced with me. The love I had received on this trip was a love to be shared.

The next secular work project was to fill a request for a heating and air conditioning company that required someone with know how to straighten out their bookkeeping system while reconciling their banking and training the secretary to do the tasks in house. This was a "work your-self out of a job" scenario, but it was a job for now. It would pay benefits I could not see well into the future. The good news was that we had an income and we settled into our rental home in a nice neighborhood. This house would stand strong and never seemed to lose power even when we rode out a hurricane. Part of the neighborhood flooded, part lost power and trees fell on houses down the street killing one person, but we were completely unscathed. God was with us. The boys loved the neighborhood and the more rural surroundings which they took full advantage of.

As my temporary job once again began to wind down after two or three months the agency sent me to a business just down the street. There I met a young man who was wrestling a flooring business into the area of success. He was amazingly sharp and quite determined. He hired me to do his books and run his crews. I was on a try out basis, but eventually he would make my position permanent. As I did everywhere I worked, I did my job as unto the Lord and He blessed me. Whatever area I was asked to step into, I did so. I learned the flow and then took charge of making it work. Once again this would bring me into contact with a variety of people from sales representatives selling the stores wares, to installation people doing the actual application in the buildings, customers and the boss.

As I progressed in my new position I was tracked down by the man who ran the air conditioning company. He requested that I come in again to help them with some problems they were still having with the banking process. He was an aggressive entrepreneur and had more than one venture percolating but it was causing complications in the check tracking. I said I would come in on a Saturday to look at what he was talking about and see what we could do to smooth it out. This would turn into a few Saturdays and then Saturday once a month to independently verify the bank reconciliation and check flow. It was too much for the secretary to keep up with as she had so many duties assigned to her already. I had a second income source that would last for the remainder of the time we would be in the area. Praise God!

So the good was being manifest for us in a marvelous way. Once established we determined we would revisit the ministry that had rejected us on the last go around. We still had that love that God had instilled in us for the preacher that had not wavered. We still watched his program and prayed for him. We came in and sat toward the back. It didn't take one of the security team long to spot us, though I had grown a beard. I wasn't trying to disguise myself. Good grief, my wife and sons were with me and she couldn't grow a beard. The guard acted as though he had a coup in his identification and spotting of me. He laughed rather sarcastically and said, "Nice beard" after slipping between the pews so he could stand directly in front of us. I just looked up and smiled and said, "Thank you. It's nice of you to notice." We weren't asked to leave.

I did not, however, overstep my bounds and continued to stay away from the altar which area I was forbidden to enter during our last sojourn to this place. Things just weren't the same this time. The music format was pretty much the same with the same basic beat we had become accustomed to. The Spirit of God did move and it was good to be able to experience that flow again. We had found the Holy Spirit few places like it was here. There were fellow Christians that we had known whom we came into contact with again. Through them and the widow lady who was still in the area, we would meet two ladies who would both write books about the events at the ministry. One I have already referenced. Both ladies had also been given a love for the preacher and the ministry. Both had insights to the workings of the inner circle. One from a position of employment and some reasonable natural discernment and the other from the spiritual side with the gifts flowing and bringing revelation one could not get from the natural view only. Amazingly, we ended up with both people continually with us in our walk for the years we would be here on this return trip… one actually living with us for a period of time.

At one point we shared the walk we were in during gatherings which suddenly began to take place in our new residence. We had learned to be cautious with whom we shared such things especially because it was hard to share something that you did not understand yourself. Yet, we proceeded as directed by the Spirit. Somehow the information reached the bowels of the ministry. Once again we were not being received by them. Let's finish my wife's testimony.

Following in quotes is my wife's written testimony continued from earlier in this writing: "In 1992 a friend of ours told us that part of the reason we were not accepted by the ministry had to do with the pregnancy. We were considered false. The day before my birthday in 1992 we went to a house meeting we had been invited to. Rita Bullock was ministering. She picked us out of a packed house jammed against a back wall and told me what I already knew. (We had never met this person before or heard of her.) She said that God was performing a miracle in my body. I had been through torment and people had said that I had made it up. Her word confirmed my walk and I held on to that for the duration of it."

"By this time I had received a personal word from the Lord concerning what was going on in my body. He said I was a sign and a wonder. In October, 1994 I started getting tired and in a couple of weeks I noticed I was getting bigger. We were in the church of a pastor now that had at one time been an instructor at the ministry. On December 4th I was noticeably pregnant. That was the day that the former pastor of the ministry was to speak at our church. Another very skeptical friend from the ministry was also in attendance. The Lord had set this up for them to see. My husband and I thought this was finally it. I was going to deliver. But after a couple of months of remaining the same size, I began to get smaller again. We were very disappointed and ready to give up on the whole thing. God's grace sustained us with confirmations and got us through."

"In 1995, I cried out to God because I was so tired of my condition, of looking like I did and the clothes I had to wear. The Spirit said He was going to make me smaller to be an even greater miracle. I remember being upset about that because I didn't want anything to hurt the babies. But over the next two or three months He did exactly what He said. There was still movement and I still had the promise. My husband would marvel at the kicking and feel around on my stomach declaring 'here's one head and here's another one. One is turned upside down from the other'. On occasion he would laugh when I positioned myself up against his back with my belly and say, 'They're kicking the old man in the butt just like the other two did.' I would enjoy a year and a half of my new size."

"The Lord started speaking to me in the summer of 1996 telling me I would be released soon. In fact I started getting bigger in October. I gave part of the testimony at church…the part people could accept. Satan really hammered me about my small size. He declared we would be upset again. One day I was so angry with God that I yelled at the ceiling that I was His daughter, too, and where was my mercy? Later that morning as I was reading I heard the Spirit say in a small voice 'You are my daughter and you shall obtain the promise'. Yes. I am His daughter and I shall obtain the promise. This whole pregnancy is not normal. It has obvious spiritual connections and is manifesting in the physical at the same time. I know the names we were given and they declared what was being done. The names are Seth Samuel and Sarah Judith. Seth: the replacement church. Samuel: dedicated unto the Lord. Sarah: a princess (pure and holy). Judith: full of praise unto God. This represented the spiritual birth of the latter day church of signs and wonders. God's replacement church, dedicated unto Him, pure and holy and full of praise for His name."

As time progressed, the folks who rented us the house found I could do bookkeeping and, though the lady had things well under control, she taught me her system and they found an excuse to pay me to help us out in our situation. The pay at my regular job was reasonable but not that great. It also came time for them to sell the house that we were in as that was the way they were building up funds to retire to their beloved Costa Rica. We began to search for a home feeling that this time we were released to buy. Once again God used my wife to give us direction leading us across the river to a home in an older neighborhood. She saw the address on the house when we passed by it. "That's the number the Lord spoke to me," she said. "That's our house."

We would find that this was a corporate sell for an employee who had been moved. Once again we had little money, a lower income and a less than exemplary history. We scraped together some earnest money to hold the house while our credit was evaluated. The representative for the corporation sat at the meeting we were in and he was incensed declaring that we were unnecessarily tying up the house. We had no business trying to buy it. Our representative declared we had made a legitimate offer, which was a good deal less than the asking price and we had our earnest money. We smiled at our adversary and I said, "That's our house. It will all work out." He left angry.

Three days later we heard from our real estate agent that the corporation had accepted our offer. Three weeks later our finances were approved. We would move once again. Here we would remain until the Lord ended our assignment in this place.

From this location, which our sons absolutely loved, we would find ourselves led to a variety of churches. God would continue to grow us showing us the good, the bad and the ugly. I will recall only two instances of several. First, we stopped in at a church that everyone was telling us we should visit. "It is so powerful," they declared. It wasn't far from home so we thought we would check it out. The preacher had some notoriety as a leader in the community. As we arrived and were identified as "new" we found ourselves escorted to the front row of the church. I don't like to start off there but I submitted myself to the ushers seating arrangement. The service started and immediately everyone in the place started running around the perimeter of the seating area. It was not all in the spirit. It was orchestrated and we were looked at rather askance because we didn't jump up and join in. Then the preaching started. It was full of shouting, spit and error. At one point the preacher shouted, "If some woman walks through that door with red lipstick all over her face I will personally take that whore and throw her out of the building!" to which everyone was shouting "Amen!" My oldest son, who was about 14 at this time, spoke up rather loudly and said from down the row, "Dad! That is absolutely wrong!" The preacher heard him and looked at me. I looked at my son and said, "Shhh! I know! We'll leave just as soon as this man is done." I did not get a very good look. The devil was in the house.

We attended another church in another small city east of us for a while at the invitation of one of my flooring installers who had found the Lord. It was a nice church with an on target pastor. There was a woman who seemed to give a "tip toe through the tulips" positive word that "everything is wonderful and God loves everybody" loudly declared exhortation every week. I began to sense that God was not pleased with it, but I did not know why. Being used in this area on occasion, but not having the word of the week so to speak, that mantle came on me during one service to speak out. What came out was a strong word of correction with a declaration that repentance was needed. The woman spoken of jumped up at the end of it and looked back at me in a rage. She proceeded to give another of her flowery words staring me down the whole time. Her actions were definitely not of the Lord. I had obviously been rebuked by her and challenged as well. I held my peace and the service continued. The pastor caught me after the service and declared that I had been right on target. He had people in the church who were vandalizing his home, his vehicle and other property trying to drive him out. They didn't like his preaching. He wanted us to stay, but I said God had already shown us to move on to a new place. I would keep him in prayer.

The new place would be a new start up under the headship again of a former professor at the bible college we had attended so long ago. Here I would be ushered once again into the position of worship leader. There was no one else to assume this mantle. It was a small contingent of 10 – 15 people transplanted from the ministry of the aforementioned preacher who were desirous of sitting under this man's anointed teaching on grace. His messages were deep and full of riches. He asked only one thing of me as I led worship and that was that I would change the wording of the songs we sang to make them more personal. It was a quirk he had which I had no problem with and I did as instructed changing "we" to "I", etc.

One evening, as I rehearsed with a new found piano player that had joined me over the previous two or three weeks, the charge to do this was completely and inadvertently forgotten as we worked on the material for the praise service. I remember saying as it grew late, "We're not done. There is one more song but I just can't connect with it." I always prayed about what songs to use and what order to sing them in. The Holy Spirit would always put it all together. The piano player chimed up with, "There is a song that has been on my heart all day. Can

I play it for you?" I said, "Yes. Please do." She began to play and it was the song! It was perfect. We added it, put it in order and ran through the songs. It had a beautiful flow. We left quite happy.

During the service the next day we had a marvelous time of praise with many compliments at the end of service. However, I noticed that our usually loving, docile preacher seemed upset and hostile as he preached on this day. After the service he angrily called me into his office. I looked at my wife and shrugged. I had no idea why he was upset. Once in his office the door was closed and he let go a tirade directed at my lack of submission and my outright rebellion in going against his wishes with the music. Still not having a clue I said, "Everyone loved the worship. We're getting compliments. What are you talking about?" This only enraged him further and he said, "You purposely usurped my authority with the worship. You went against everything I have put in place and did not change the wording as I have told you to do!" He was shouting. Now the light finally lit. He was right. I hadn't changed the words. I had totally spaced it off. It was not intentional. But to make things worse I said, "I did not mean to do this. It was an accident. What difference does it make? If God gave the song to the writer the way it was written don't you suppose it was still pleasing to Him?" That was the wrong thing to say. It got louder and a bit offensive. Finally I held up my hands and declared I would not be talked to in this manner by anyone. If he was convinced my error was intentional then we would leave it at that. My family and I would not be back. Everyone in the place heard what went on.

Another Sunday passed and we did not attend. Two weeks later I received a phone call from the preacher during which I was accused of having called up everyone in his church to turn them against him. His count which had grown to around sixty had dropped to 8-10 the following week and the week after no one showed. He shut the church down. I made it clear that I had spoken to no one since leaving. His problem was not with me. He didn't believe me.

You don't mess with what God is doing. The Holy Spirit directed me in what to do and how to do it as I took on this task and gave it my best. I believe that the "spacing off" of the charge of the preacher to change the music wording was the Holy Spirit laying a challenge at this man's feet. He had raised an idol in his life without knowing it and because he did he came against the anointing the Spirit of God blessed me with for the music. There was a price. Do not touch God's anointed or come against what He has established. The true sign of a Christian man is that he can ultimately be corrected. One year later in a parking lot outside of a grocery store I heard a familiar voice call to me. I turned to see this preacher whom I had not spoken to since the day he called me accusing me. He asked for my forgiveness for what had taken place. I gave it quickly. He asked me to visit a new church he was starting up in his house. I had to decline as we were at that time planted in another place. We wished one another well and parted reunited in the Spirit.

The years had passed and our parents had reached older age with the ensuing physical problems that can come. My Dad was quite ill over the period of time we were back in Louisiana with lung problems suffering several lung collapses. This had caused us three rush "if you want to see your Dad alive you had better hurry" trips to Nebraska....a 26 hour straight through drive. On the next to the last trip when I would see my Dad we were half way there when the Lord said he would be alright. "Why did you not tell me and save me the trip?" We arrived in the middle of the night and went through the emergency entrance. We were told that we would have to come back during visiting hours. I related how long I had been on the road and I requested just a few moments for us to look in on Dad and we would come back the next day. It was allowed. We went into the room and I hugged Dad. He had tubes all over his body. I told him he was going to make it and we would see him later that day.

Once rested, my Mom and our family all headed for the hospital. We visited for a while and my wife began to discuss salvation with my parents....a visit we had many times before but without much success. They acquainted our efforts I suppose with our strange walk and lifestyle. That tended to close their ears to us. The present circumstances and the improved condition of our lives seemed to open them up to us on this journey. They asked questions. Both knew of God but had never asked Jesus to come into their heart. They were good people but heaven was not their destination at this juncture. We explained the personal need to declare Jesus to be Lord, accept His death and shed blood as the full payment for their sins and know that He had been raised from the dead as a promise to all who came to Him that they would be raised up with Him to a new life. Praise God! They asked to pray the prayer of salvation with us and received Jesus Christ as savior in the hospital room that morning! I then looked at my Dad and I said, "You are going to get up out of this bed and go home. It is not time for you to leave yet." Two days later, before we left town, I watched the nurse wheel him out of the hospital to the waiting car to go home. He would live one more year.

I had moved from the carpet store job through another difficult period of no work that put us behind on our house payment. During this time frame I awakened one night to see a white ethereal being standing about 15 feet from me in the doorway of our bedroom. The image was wrapped in a white robe also of ethereal nature like a dull white light. As I watched I found myself beginning to relax from the initial shock and the being moved towards me in a gentle fashion. When it was about half way to me it began to dance slowly, then more in a side to side prancing motion. As it did so I felt that extremely powerful crushing force come against me that I had experienced before. I was knocked to the mattress and immediately began to cry out "Jesus" as the figure ripped back the robe of light revealing a hideous demonic figure. My wife was awakened by my struggle and threw her hand to my forehead declaring the blood of Jesus. The figure departed. The Lord then showed me I had just experienced the deception of the angel of light spirit that had been and was attacking his churches. He had shown me the fruits of that in many of the churches he had taken us to and He was displeased that they were so easily overcome.

I overheard my air conditioning part time bookkeeping employer one Saturday commiserating with his brother over the problems they were having getting a service department running efficiently. There were a lot of headaches and they were more oriented to construction and installation. Service was a nuisance, but necessary. I asked for the job.

"You are a bookkeeper. What would you know about a service department?" My previous history of wholesale heating and air conditioning controls, commercial temperature controls and system design, heating and air conditioning systems and that I had run service departments before came to light. While skeptical, I was known for my work ethic and honesty. I was to be given a shot at it. There is really no need to go into detail here except to say the service business was blessed by God as I sought His help and it grew exponentially in one year. It was so successful with a positive customer satisfaction feedback that my employer would openly admit he was praying that my house would not sell when advised I had to get back closer to home in case our parents needed us.

Part of that truth was that I had one of my experiences during which I awakened to see a vision of Texas raised up out of a relief map. I saw a meteor like object fly across the sky with a football team's emblem on it and saw it hit the ground in a mighty explosion. A friend said I saw the shuttle blowing up before it happened. Some say I have seen an event yet to happen. Perhaps I saw an asteroid trailing this passing Comet Elenin striking the earth in this area. Others think it may be a spiritual revival breaking out. I hope it is the latter. I don't know. I did hear a voice that declared that one was coming out of Southwest Texas like a whirlwind to take care of my financial situation. Having been through that area on our honeymoon I protested that "there was nothing in Southwest Texas but empty fields on one side and sagebrush on the other." The voice spoke again in a very firm tone and repeated the message. By then I was up on one elbow and was so impacted by the tone all I could say was, "Yes, Lord." To date that remains on the shelf as a seventeen year promise. God has his people everywhere.

We made a trip to the north Texas area to search out the land and finally felt led to a little town northwest of Fort Worth. I'm not sure how we found it except to say that God used my wife again. We didn't find a place to live but we returned to our home believing it was once again sold. Some folks had declared their intent to buy it but needed a month or two to put things together. They turned out to be false and it caused us some problems which our friend Patricia Sunday had to help us with since we were so far away. We ultimately did get the house sold to someone else.

Prior to our move there was a nice going away celebration held for me at the air conditioning company and during the party I had a lot of money placed in my hands to help my family out. This was a blessing as I really had no money to make this move. It would sustain us for three months.

My father had passed away before we could get moved. There would be times when I wondered if I had gotten out of God's will. Yet, He provided for us once again after a period of difficulty which I will cover in the next chapter. It would be during this time of transition that I would feel the intercessory call for the preacher at the ministry, who had been embattled for so many years, lift from me. Within my spirit I heard that it was no longer necessary to continue. There had been a victory. I have not kept up with or watched this man on television since that time. There would be one trip to Louisiana to return a trailer we lived in when we stopped in to see what God was doing around 1999. That stop only confirmed that we were no longer connected the way we had been.

I drove the moving truck with our accumulated goods and my wife followed in the van we had purchased as the Nova had finally given up the ghost. The most difficult part of this move occurred when my oldest son refused to move again. He had a lot of friends, liked it where we were and he was staying. He was of age. It was his choice. I watched him in the side mirror as we drove off and my heart was breaking. I stopped frequently as we drove towards our new home to give my wife rest. We stopped just over the border in Texas at a rest area and sat at a picnic table having our lunch. We had no idea where we were moving to as we had nothing secured once again. We smiled at one another not knowing that we would be challenged for a few months to survive in our new location…and I held her hand.

Chapter 9
OUR FAITH IS TRIED

Texas greeted us with a dingy little motel room which would serve as our base of operations for two or three days while we scouted out a place to move to. This is what is called a move of faith. Once again we knew the area to search out but the specific place to move to had not been identified. We had to have a quick answer. I could only keep the moving van for so long. Then it would be rental storage time. God worked a marvelous miracle of provision for us before we left Louisiana and we had the money to get a place to live.

We drove into our future home city with the moving van and our own van fully expecting to be successful on the first day. I parked the van outside of a residential area in front of a vacant lot near a medical facility so we could more easily go into the area to look at prospective homes. Once again, my wife felt this was the area to look in. We did not know that we could see our new location from where I parked but we were blinded to it. None of the places we looked at connected with us. We returned to the moving van to find a street crew and the police gathered around it. It turned out that the street crew was scheduled to resurface the roadway where I had parked that morning. We also found that there was an ordinance in the city prohibiting parking on the street as I had done. We had to open up the moving van and allow a brief inspection to verify our story. We received many strange looks from one and all when they realized how far we had come with no place to stay. I asked where I could legally park the moving van to stay out of trouble. The officer investigating was kind enough to refer me to a couple of places, one of which we used the next day.

The following day we contacted a local real estate company that handled some rental properties. We looked at two or three and they were less than acceptable. We asked the Lord what to do and where He wanted us. At last, we were led to the duplex which was a short distance across the field from where I had originally parked the truck. We paid our deposit and our first month rent and moved in. We had every confidence that I would soon be working and everything would be fine. After all, we'd been through all the tests. There surely was no need for us to have to go through any more rigorous trials. (Let it be stated here that trials are those things that work out patience in us. God has His timing in all things and our submission to that is often times preceded by a trial that involves our timetable versus His.)

We loved our new location. It wasn't a long drive to a local lakefront park and we had a great neighborhood to go for evening walks in. As we had searched for a place to live we passed by a little church that drew my wife in. She was certain that we were to begin our journey in that place. We attended the next Sunday and found a small group of very nice people who loved the Lord. We would be there for a period of time and they would stand with us as we wrestled with the challenges that were ahead.

One of the major obstacles to total contentment was finding employment. I searched out the employment sections and put in applications but could not seem to get to first base. I couldn't get connected through the usual temporary service entities I had used before either. After a couple of months things were looking rough. I had been able to pick up some work at a local machine shop through the pastor of the church which we now attended. The pastor picked up side work there to help out with his bills. It was a total learning experience as I had never done anything like this before. The man who ran the shop was an easy going individual who was willing to teach. He understood my situation and tried to give me what work he could, but he could only pay minimum wage. I ran his machines for many hours, often times working all night to finish projects. He trusted me immediately and gave me a key to the place so I could come out and work whenever I wanted to. I would also find he was in desperate need of having his books put in order. I would eventually pick this up as some side work which would lead to four or five bookkeeping accounts for me that generated additional money every month. Unfortunately it was not enough to save us. Our money ran out and the real estate company allowed us to stay to use up the one month deposit but they had no choice but to ask us to move on. We had kept them fully informed as to our situation and they were exceedingly kind to us.

It was at this point that we would find ourselves sleeping on the floor of the church for about a week. From this location we would be invited by some people who knew our pastor to move into a house that would be sitting vacant as the man was getting married and moving to another state. I thought we were being asked to stay until the house sold. I was told there was some fix up and cleaning to be done and that he would on occasion try to slip in to do that. I worked around the yard to gather the fall debris, bagged a lot of it and it was hauled off. I also tried to isolate the owner's personal furniture from our use of the house into one room we were not using. Somewhere in this effort I apparently functioned with complete misunderstanding of the arrangement and found that, while he was kind, the owner was upset with our nesting in and made it clear we were to find another location.

Fortunately, during this time frame I had obtained a better paying job. It wasn't much more than minimum wage and certainly did not respect my capabilities initially but it was a regular full time job. It just takes a while to get caught up when you have fallen behind. These temporary living quarters had allowed us the time we needed. I remember driving past the work place that would be my second home for the next 13 ½ years, pointing to it while passing by (as I had applied there) and saying to the Lord, "You control all things! It is nothing for you to get me a job there so I don't have to drive all the way to Fort Worth every day!" I received a call two days later to come in for an interview. Another two days and I was advised that the job was mine. Praise God! I would start November 17th, 1997 and work until I retired on April 21, 2011. This would be the longest running job I had ever

not be a defeat but would glorify God. We spoke to every aspect of what the doctor had reported to us and declared God's full restoration healing and power. This medical report was made available to the ever growing prayer chain. We stayed the night and waited for the morning news from the doctor.

Once again the doctor joined us and said the surgery was now postponed. There had been a significant reduction in the swelling. They would continue to monitor Aaron throughout the day for any changes. We were allowed to see him briefly. Many people stopped in to see us as we waited and prayed with us. Later in the afternoon the doctor returned to tell us that our son was being moved to a room because he was showing good improvement. There would be no surgery. We were allowed to go to the room where a nurse was tending to Aaron. The doctor told us that we should expect Aaron to be in a coma for at least three months while his brain healed. There was damage to the area of the brain that would affect his memory and would give him future problems with reasoning. Once he woke up we needed to be aware that he might not even remember us. Again we addressed these things to the Lord and called upon his healing power to bring restoration to our son's body.

We stood over his bed, anointed him with oil and declared our faith. The nurse looked at us and said, "You are exhausted. There is nothing more you can do here. The best thing you can do for your son is to go home and get some rest. I will call you if there is any change." We left our phone number with the nurse and took her advice. Once home we cleaned up, advised our other sons of their brother's prognosis, present condition and collapsed into bed. The next morning we received a phone call. It was the nurse. She was just going off duty and had to call. She very excitedly said, "Guess who is sitting in a chair next to his bed while I put clean sheets on it?" Praise God for miracles!

On our first visit to the hospital that day we spent three hours in our sons room greeting the various visitors who came in as he was no longer in intensive care but in a regular room. I remember standing in the hallway as the young man walked by who had been with Aaron and allowed Aaron to use his motorcycle. He asked if he could go in. I told him to go ahead as our son was talking to everyone. He recognized all who came and had no trouble in that area. The young man went in and came right back out. He said that our son was wondering why we hadn't been in to see him yet. Were we coming in? I advised him that we had just stepped out after being in the room for quite a long time but we would be back in shortly. The short term memory problems the doctor told us would occur were manifesting. The reasoning functions we all take for granted also would manifest and life would be faced with numerous challenges from poor choices down the road. I can't explain why God didn't heal this basic brain function with everything else, but we rejoiced in what He did do.

I was approached after a day or two by a surgeon who had looked at Aaron's x-rays when asked to by the brain surgeon to evaluate the facial fractures. He advised me that it would be necessary to put a plate in our son's face to repair the damage and minimize disfigurement. After my wife and I prayed about it and studied our son's face, we felt very strongly that God was telling us "No." We declined the procedure. Our son received his touch from God in this area as well and has no problems or disfigurement.

There was a point in time during all of this when I became quite angry with Satan attacking my son. Remembering his threats and knowing I had been released from my previous assignment of intercession and the experiences I had related to that, I faced him without fear in the spirit realm and declared that he would never touch my son again. This was my new intercession. He would have to go through me first.

Our time in our nice little home appeared to be coming to an end. The estate was settled and the family wanted to move on a sale. I had no down payment money and could not get a loan. We would once again face a difficult housing period in our lives. Our friend Patricia Sunday had a 16 foot camper trailer she offered to us for our use until we could work something else out. I declared that I was not going to live in a camper trailer. No way! She followed the leading of the Spirit and pulled it all the way from Baton Rouge anyway. We would live in it for eight months and two days. The hardest part of this time period, which was absolutely crushing for me and my wife, involved the necessity of our middle son moving in with the family of one of his close friends from school. We simply could not all fit in the trailer as it only had a three foot by six foot aisle with bunk beds on one end and a table on the other. He was well on his way to 6' 5". We did have a cook stove and a little window unit that I bought but it still got hot in the afternoon once we got to summer. We parked it in a little marina near the lake and took up residence.

We met a lot of nice people and lived with the humbling experience that was before us in this venue. Our move in occurred during the early part of the year with our furniture going to a storage facility. The marina struggled with the hot water system, which we were susceptible to having no facilities in the camper. Each day we had to walk the 75 yards or so to the public use facilities for bathroom duties and showers. Our adventure here had begun in January and many times we had to jump in and out of cold water on cold days to try to wash up. It was a blessing when the boiler was finally fixed. The cottonwoods were great by the lake and afforded some relief in what turned out to be a challenging summer of heat.

My wife had met some people at a church we felt led to visit and had joined them in working at a food distribution center for the needy. With their help we would eventually hold a singing and gospel presentation under the cottonwoods for our neighbors. There would be a tent meeting at another location in town. We met a lot of people hungry for more of the Lord. It was during this time that a young man was introduced as a man of real fire for the Lord. He could play the piano and sing so he was welcomed in by the little mission church. He would be an asset they thought for the meetings they held in various outdoor locations. The first time my wife and I experienced his ministry we looked at each other and said, "Something is definitely not right here." It was held up as a mighty thing that this man would become so full of the spirit he would hammer the keys on his piano until his fingers bled. He was full of the spirit all right…a demonic spirit. I tried to subtly point this out to the leadership but they determined I was wrong and would not hear.

At an outdoor meeting at a local small town this man was invited to speak and play. I moved away from the group to a location across the parking lot and began to walk and pray for the service. I began to bind up the spirit that was in this man. I was a good distance away praying in tongues so he could not hear me, yet he did and he began to scream into the microphone at me causing everyone to turn and look in my direction. As this man continued to spew accusations and names in my direction tremendous calm engulfed me and I began to walk toward him. The closer I got the more he raged. I walked up and took the microphone out of his hand, looked him in the eye and shouted, "You foul spirit from hell! I command you to shut up in Jesus name!" His response was to run away weeping. A lady ran after him to console him and she would paint me as the bad guy later coming strongly against me demanding my removal from all activities with the mission church. She was stricken with an ailment that confined her to bed. I never saw this young man again. I hope he got set free.

We moved away from the church we had begun in and joined with a church in another city that had some mission outreaches going into Mexico. Once again I found myself being asked to sing as the folks at the little food mission my wife worked with had learned from her I had experience. They had been utilizing me for that in the mission's services. They told the people at the church which they also attended. This resulted in me being asked to go on the next mission trip to Mexico. There was room for one more and, while my wife wanted to go, we felt that one of us had to stay home with the boys. As it turned out we had contact with our friend Patricia Sunday about this time and she became the last disciple for the journey.

This would be a memorable journey as we joined with two other churches in the effort and each would have a night to head up the services in the little village we were headed for. The English translation for the name of the village was "the city of no water". Probably the most significant event I remember occurred the night the pastor we were associated with was scheduled to preach. We began with the usual sparse seating in the area of chairs that had been set up. I wondered why so much effort had been put in to such a seemingly unpopulated village in the middle of nowhere, but God is concerned with one lost lamb. As the preacher presented the gospel, clouds formed in the distance which was an unusual event for this desert area. We were told that the rain didn't get past the mountain range we were looking at where the clouds formed. We didn't need to worry about it disrupting the meeting. As the service continued the cloud bank grew and continued a slow approach. The preacher closed as a gentle rain began to fall. Three or four people came forward for prayer which almost emptied our chairs and we dutifully moved forward to minister to them. The rain then began to fall in a gentle mist and as it did the Spirit of God fell in that place with power. Darkness had fallen at the end of the meeting from a natural standpoint but we were suddenly standing in a great light spiritually. To this day I do not know where the people came from, but they had all been in the shadows listening. When the Spirit fell we experienced what Christ experienced when it says in the bible that he was thronged by the people. We were surrounded on all sides by a multitude of people reaching their hands out to us and crying out for prayer. We could not move for several minutes because of the crush of the people. It was an extraordinary experience!

We had met some highly dedicated Mexican nationals who had joined us for this ministry outreach. They traveled with whatever the Lord provided them and were extremely helpful in carrying forward the gospel on this occasion. I was privileged to spend a good deal of time with them and they had a lot of fun trying to teach me some basic Spanish so I could minister. They recounted many instances of hardship and danger that they had endured but the smiles never left their faces. God had saved them out of their sinful lifestyles and they had become true disciples of the Master.

Coming home to what would be an impending move to the Marina previously mentioned had me counting my blessings as I shared with my wife what I had seen regarding living conditions where we had been. She rejoiced with me as I shared with her the spiritual explosion we had witnessed on our last night in Mexico. She would be scheduled to go on the next journey but events would transpire outside of our control that would prevent that. She was truly disappointed.

The company I worked for started a program for educational training of the personnel involved in sales. I decided to take advantage of it as there was a thousand dollar bonus for successful completion of all phases of the course. I dug into it whole heartedly as a thousand dollars was a lot of money. At the end of the course I received a certificate and the money which we immediately decided to use to get out of the camper and into a better place. The only avenue open to us seemed to be with the mobile home manufacturer sales divisions which were big at the time. It was advertised that you could get into a new home on an acre of land for $1,000.00 down. We had the money and we started looking. We found the home we are in and my wife declared it was the one we were to get. The salesperson kept pressing us to buy another unit which was much lower in quality. My wife shook her head in the negative and I declared it to the salesperson. He said he really couldn't work out a deal on what my wife wanted and he once again tried to push us to the one he wanted to sell us. The salesperson left the room again to negotiate with the supervisor. I leaned over to my wife and I told her to follow my lead. When the salesperson returned it was the same old song with a slightly different tune. I looked the person squarely in the eye and very nicely said, "I appreciate all of your efforts on our behalf. The people down the street have a similar double wide trailer which we also like and they were ready to deal. It's much better quality than what you are trying to sell me. I've told you I'm not interested in anything but the trailer you showed us earlier that my wife likes. If you won't sell me that then we are leaving." With that we got up, walked out the door and across the parking lot with sad faces on my sons who wanted this home. My wife was repeating to me that she knew we were to get this particular home. I said, "I know. Just trust God." We were getting in the car to leave when a shout stopped us. "We figured out a way we can make this happen. We can get you into the trailer you want!" Oh, how I hate games. But I had told them the truth. We could have purchased the other trailer. All we had to do was go sign the papers down the street. God gave my wife the desire of her heart and the floor plan she liked.

Our eight month ordeal was about to end. We selected our lot and I mowed down the area where we wanted our double wide placed. We were so excited that our living arrangement would soon be changed. Our whole family was going to be back together once again. The son who had lived with another family was coming home. Our feelings of being the worst parents in the world would eventually be put to rest. It would turn out that the father of my son's friend would hire him as a mechanic once he finished trade school and had paid a few dues for experience. What we saw as a horrendous failure on our part that caused us much grief worked to the good for our son.

There it was. We were looking at our new home. Everything was set, hooked up and the long wait for it all to come together was over. We walked in the front door and rejoiced that it was ours. We praised and thanked our God for His provision for us and deliverance from difficult circumstances. He was faithful. It was October. After two years of struggle to get established in this state we were finally settling in. We would live in this house together for eleven years. Our love continued to be made stronger by all that we endured together. God was increasing our faith. It would be hard for me to look back on all of this and know that not long after this miracle of provision I would once again begin to lose my way.

But for now, we had a home again. This battle was won. God had brought the victory. We stood in the kitchen looking out the window at our acre of ground. We smiled so big at each other I thought our faces would break…and I held her hand.

Chapter 10
ANOTHER GENERATION

Life in our new home was such a blessing to us. I didn't particularly enjoy mowing this acre of ground with a push mower, but from a cardiovascular standpoint God would use it to keep me in top condition. That was a good thing as I would become subject to attack a short time later. As it was now, we could focus on our two youngest sons finishing their high school careers. Our oldest had dropped out but would later return to get his GED. We had for the first time in a long time some semblance of a normal life. Go to work, go to church, attend school activities and come home to family. Wow! Did everybody get to live this blessing?

Time passed with graduations and we would see our two youngest leave the fold, get an apartment together and take advantage of programs offered in our state for further education through technical schools. Both had decided on auto mechanics and, while the older of the two had graduated two years before, he had remained undecided about his direction until the two of them went forward in the area stated. Their graduation from this school would involve them in some entry level "dues paying" jobs for a while which they stuck with until the door opened for better things. Our oldest son moved from job to job struggling to find himself as a result of residual problems from his head injury. There would be times he would leave the house heading for one place and we would find he ended up somewhere completely different. It was hard for him to understand the requirements for consistency on the job and no amount of reasoning seemed to penetrate his thinking. There wasn't any job he couldn't handle physically or mentally. He was easily distracted or led astray. It was just going to take time for this aspect of his being to heal.

The connection we had with the little church in the other city broke down over the previously mentioned incident and it would finally close later. I was becoming frustrated with the constant turmoil not knowing what was lying just ahead and I decided that I was done with all of these church battles. We had new neighbors all around and my wife hit the neighborhood sharing her love for the Lord with any who would listen. There weren't many. However, our next door neighbors got after us to hold services in our house which we would do for about a year and a half until they moved away. We had other occasional visitors but typically had no more than 6 – 10 people in attendance. Our neighbor lady did receive salvation so it was not a wasted effort by any means. Perhaps my expectations were too high or my motivation wasn't lined up properly with the Lord's plan for my life at this time. Through this process I became disenchanted with the price versus the results that I was judging fell short of the "explosion" I wanted to be part of. (I allude to the vision I had seen in a previous chapter.) I got full of myself. The Lord told me to shut down our house ministry. I also set my bible aside and stopped my daily reading. I would not attend any church during this time. Basically I said, "Here I am devil. Give me your best shot. I don't care anymore. Things aren't going the way I want them to. I'm defeated."

My enemy accepted the invitation I had extended. He came right over and took up residence all around whispering in my ear, tempting me and promising me pleasures if I would bow my knee to him. Most of it I shook off as I did have an anchor in my soul that engaged in this battle for me as I was too weak to lift a finger to help myself. But my outward actions revealed that I had returned to the inner weakness to try to find peace in my life. My temper was not under control. I would visit that place often and find momentary peace, but little satisfaction. I even accused God saying, "I warned you to take this thorn from my flesh and all you ever said was 'my grace is sufficient'. Look at me now. Where is your grace?" My wife stayed by my side and I was honest with her about these struggles going on in me. She encouraged me to stand strong and she would stand with me. She understood more than I did at the time the attack I was under. We continued to pray together. I remained in this state for several months blaming everything and everybody for my problems. I was sick of trying to reach out to unresponsive people and now I had become one. It says in the bible "your sin will find you out." I came to a new understanding of that scripture. It isn't about the world finding out and persecuting you over it, though that typically happens….and did. It is that when the sin you have hidden away is revealed to you that you find yourself exposed to the truth and you surrender that part of yourself to the Lord admitting your inability to handle it or it will ultimately destroy you. Well, it found me out in the latter sense and I hated what I saw. I was ashamed that I knew so much and I still thought I could find peace going to this place instead of turning to the Lord and giving the burden to Him. But the Spirit drew me, arrested me once again and I found that desire welling up in me to have fellowship with believers. We attended a local church one Sunday and sat in the back row. My head rested up against the back wall as I listened to this young preacher declare the gospel. While this church was not functional in all of the gifts as their doctrine spoke against those things, the Spirit of God still moved in that place for me that day and I felt myself being enclosed in a cylinder. It filled with an odor that broke down all of my hardness. I wept openly but quietly as the Spirit of God began to restore me. We would attend here for quite a while until the Lord moved us to a church more open to the full operation of the gifts of the Spirit.

This unfortunate time frame in my walk also bore a price. We had a difficult allergy season and I had the worst year I can ever remember. At one point I felt so weak I finally went to the doctor at my wife's insistence. I was ushered into a room and waited until the nurse came for the initial evaluation and taking of vitals. She looked at me rather strangely and asked if I felt ok. I responded that I was feeling rather weak. She left and I prepared myself for the expected wait until the doctor could get to me on his rounds. Thirty seconds later the door burst open and the doctor stood looking at me with an expression of deep concern. He said, "Are you feeling alright?" I responded again that I felt weak, but other than that ok. He said, "You shouldn't even be sitting here." Now he had my attention. He said, "Your blood pressure is awfully low." I said, "It is always a little low. That's normal for me." "No," he said, "it's 88 over 65. You are badly dehydrated and it is dangerous." Whoa! The physical attack came with the spiritual attack. He wanted to put me in the hospital but I declined. I was given a prescription to get filled immediately and I was told to drink lots of water and other fluids. I was to get started immediately and come back in to get checked. I did what I was told.

As I stood at the sales counter at work the next day the dehydration from allergies, the reduced blood pressure and a sudden severe headache (migraine style) combined to restrict blood flow to the left side of my head for just a moment in time. That is all it took. My physician would later identify a TIA stroke. In that moment the damage was done. I was in the middle of a sentence when I could no longer speak correctly slurring my words. I began to lose my equilibrium but somehow managed to stay on my feet. My associate recognized that I was having problems and called the warehouse manager to the front to take me home. I finally managed to get out that I wanted them to call my wife and take me to the emergency room.

Once at the hospital I was rushed into the ER area and hooked up to an EKG machine. I was having trouble explaining what had happened as I still could not speak. I looked up and said, "God. I don't know what is happening to me, but you do. Please keep me in the palm of your hand. I place myself in your hands right now. Do not leave me!" A doctor came in and began checking me over. Again I had trouble communicating my situation. My youngest son came in as my wife had called him. She had no car and no way to get to me. I was being wheeled in for a CAT scan. The results of the blood work, the EKG, the CAT scan and a couple of other tests that were run came back. The doctor entered the space I was in which was surrounded by drapes and he was angry. I was baffled. He started pounding on one side of my body, then on the other asking, "Does this feel the same?" I was saying as best I could slur out, "No." He remained highly agitated. He must have thought I was on drugs or something. I don't know. He said, "There is absolutely nothing wrong with you! All of your tests show you to be in perfect health. You are wasting my time. You need to go home."

My son carried me out to his waiting car as I had no ability to use my right side. I was, however, in perfect health. I had just been chastised for not demonstrating any verifiable symptoms. I just thanked God that He had already started answering my prayer before I could pray it and my body was being restored from this attack. I would return to work one week later as I could not afford to stay home any longer. My vacation was used up and my company had no sick leave provisions. Everyone I encountered suggested that I go back home but I stood in the healing that was going on. From that day to this there is nothing that I cannot do and my speech returned within a couple of days. My personal physician did advise me that what I reported as an intense burning sensation and loss of ability to tell temperature or "feel" anything on my right side was probably a permanent result of the stroke. Further investigation of the symptoms on the internet would reveal to me that all of our nerves have little caps on the end to temper the response waves to the brain. During a stroke these caps disintegrate. They can never be fixed. Thus the sensations I was having. I have lived with this burning and lack of sense of feeling for 8 ½ years. Only recently did I receive a partial healing and reduction in the burning with some return of feeling on my right side. It is not complete, but God is not done!

My oldest son had found a friend in his circle of acquaintances that we would be introduced to on a day in June, 2002. We did not realize the extent of the relationship that was developing between the two of them. We were simply told that the young lady was headed for the street as her apartment had burned and she had nowhere to go. The complication was a 14 month old little girl that was hers. The latter melted our hearts and we said we would allow them to move in until other arrangements could be made. Separate bedrooms were dictated and the rules of conduct were explained.

As time wore on we found ourselves more in charge of this little girl than we had anticipated. The life style of Mom was fully involved in the nightly run to the bar and our son was in concert with the plan. We were upset by it as well as the daily lifestyle that involved sleeping in half the day and awakening only to sit on the couch and watch "soaps" all afternoon. Any desire for attention or maintenance of the little girl generally fell to my wife with "Mom" sending the little one away to a room and not allowing her to come out and bother her while she watched her shows. Truth was manifesting and we didn't like it much. Our problem now became what would happen to this little girl if she wasn't with us to be cared for. We were between a rock and a hard place. Then we found out there was a pregnancy underway and my son was going to be a Dad. We prayed about it and decided to ride it out until the birth of our grandchild. There was definite concern for this future child as well.

The revelations just kept coming from this lady as we found she had been involved in witchcraft and the occult. She would smuggle things into the house which we had specifically forbidden. It would irritate her when they were discovered and we would insist on the removal of whatever it was. There was a night when she came screaming across the house to our room in a total state of panic. "There are demons all over the place! Help me!" She was pounding on our door and we jumped up, grabbed our robes and went to her. I opened the door and was hit by a strong presence of evil. My wife began immediately pleading the blood of Jesus and taking authority. She picked it up instantly, too. The force was quite directional and I proceeded towards the focal point of it. As I did so I hit a wall that was a similar experience to trying to run in a swimming pool. Our daughter-in-law started screaming again. "Look at them! Look at them! They are all over the walls!" I couldn't see them but I could feel them. I moved into their bedroom to find posters and decorations that did not belong there. I also found one of those openings into darkness emanating from one of the posters of her favorite rock group who delved into the satanic darkness with their music. I anointed the room as my wife anointed the house and we took authority over these hordes and commanded them to go to the abyss to await their judgment. We were able to close the portal and some semblance of peace returned.

We prayed with our future daughter-in-law who was scared out of her wits. I explained to her again what she had managed to do and this time she ripped down the posters and symbols and asked me to destroy them. I went out into the back yard in the middle of the night and burned everything in my grill. It emitted many strange colors. When that ended we all retired to bed. I reclined for about five minutes and spoke to my wife. I said, "Don't go to sleep. It's not over. She's holding out." My wife said, "I know. I'm awake and waiting." We no sooner got that conversation ended and the running, screaming lady came back across the house. I opened the door and said, "This time I want all of it. What you held back has to go." Out came the CD's of her once favorite group and I destroyed them as well. People who don't know the Lord may get away with having this stuff around as they are already locked in to their fate. If you bring it into a Christian home the attached demons go into a rage against the light. They prefer the darkness. Be warned.

The birth occurred and we had another little girl. She was beautiful, too, and her care fell to us once again. I spent many days walking the floor with this baby as she had a lot of stomach problems. Mom hadn't taken very good care of herself during the pregnancy. This went on for a year with my wife and me providing the primary efforts. We pressed really hard about the marriage issue and would find that this young lady was still married to someone else by whom she had a son that she was not allowed to see. She had married quite young and her history of choices was consistent to this point. The little girl we had been caring for belonged to someone else whom she had never married as the prior marriage was in place at that time, too. Our son's reasoning process left him quite vulnerable and we could do little to change that, nor did we want to at this point with another child involved in the picture. These kids would need care.

With time the divorce from the outstanding marriage was completed and a wedding was planned. My son asked me to conduct the service. Since she had never had a "real wedding" our future daughter-in-law wanted the dress, the church and the things that would accompany such a gathering. We had ministered with her during this time and she was changing course but was not all the way into the commitment. Based on that we helped all we could to give the two of them a special day. It turned out to be a very nice wedding ceremony.

Not long after my son found a job in a city a good distance away and they happily moved nearer his work location into their first apartment. The house was really lonely now and despite the work involved my wife and I missed the babies. This new arrangement lasted about three months before my son's wife determined it wasn't working for her and she left. My son probably didn't help the situation a lot as he failed to understand his wife's needs. This is when we would find she had been diagnosed bi-polar and was supposed to be on medication. She also had severe asthma but smoked heavily. Smoking was not allowed in our home which my son knew as he had also picked up the addiction. The two girls had been diagnosed with asthma at this point so smoking in their apartment wasn't doing anyone any good.

At first she took the kids, but could not handle them or did not want to. We ended up with the baby but she had the older girl in tow. I received a phone call from a very depressed Mom during which she revealed she was sitting near a lake with the older girl in the car and was contemplating driving in. I looked up and said, "Help me, Lord. I need words now!" I don't remember all that was said but I did reassure her that everything would be ok. She just needed to bring me the older girl and we would try to help her out. She did as I asked. As despondent as she was she did not want to hurt her child. She did not stay with us but we had both girls safely in our home now. My son continued in his job and stayed alone in his apartment for several months as he had a lease. He would drive over and stay with us on the weekends. Finally he became lonely and asked if he could move back in to be closer to the girls.

We seldom had contact with his wife during this time frame except for the holidays or the girl's birthdays when she would show up and want them. We had concerns but we had little choice. We had no authority. My son had friends in common with her and we began to hear that drugs were becoming increasingly involved in her new life style. That became a cause of great concern. We were advised that she had no problem when she had the children of hanging out in these "houses" where drugs were being used. She had taken the girls for a while and would not bring them back again. My son encountered her and was driving them back here which she apparently figured out, panicked and dragged the kids out of the car at a busy intersection making a terrible scene. He found out where she had gone after leaving his car and went there after calling the police. They showed up at the location and my son told them his wife had his kids in an apartment where drugs were being used and he feared for their safety. He was told by the police that if he did not leave the premises he would be arrested.

Finally, she needed our help again and brought the girls back to us. We prayed a lot for their safety during this time. The stress was unbelievable but we felt God moving us in a particular direction and we stood firm. The life my son's wife was leading deteriorated and she called wanting to right her course, accept the Lord and do the right thing. We counseled with her but had to leave town for a while on a planned trip. It had become common for us to take the girls with us on our annual trip to our home state. When we returned we found Mom all moved back in. This was not supposed to be part of the deal. Once again our son's reasoning process had put a bump in our path. What could we say? They were married and had reconciled. She asked for mercy. What choice did we have? At least we knew where she was and where the girls were. Our newest revelation came one month into our new adventure when she announced her pregnancy. She was so happy in her declaration that she would give our son another child. Things actually went along pretty well for most of the year as she even attended church with us. We believed she was actually trying and outward indications seemed to confirm that.

Just prior to the return of our daughter-in-law my wife and I compared notes and we received our first spiritual tug involving a future move. It was 2004. We both had heard Florida. We had no idea how this could take place especially regarding our situation with the children we were now raising. We put this knowledge on the shelf to be dealt with at some future point. Then, with the return of our daughter-in-law, we were sure that it was well off in the future.

The time for the birth rolled around and we rejoiced to see a little boy added to the fold. One look and everyone knew that this child was not my son's. We held our peace and my son agreed to his name going on the birth certificate. All was happy until we got home. Something triggered in this woman who had just had this child. She declared in no uncertain terms that she was caring for this boy and we would not spoil him by hugging him and holding him all the time like we had the other two. Where did this come from? This baby was going to learn that his Momma needed her sleep and he was not going to bother her. I looked at my wife and we again held our peace. We monitored her actions toward this child during the next two or three weeks. The basics seemed to be getting taken care of, but she definitely was true to her word on not holding or nurturing this baby boy. Her total attitude was one of rejection. My son finally shared with us that she claimed a drug related rape.

One evening I heard the little guy fussing and crying in their bedroom. I couldn't stand it anymore and walked in. I found him soaked in milk with the bottle shoved upside down near him. He was propped up by pillows in a car seat and he was badly soiled. He was hot and sweaty. She was three feet from him and was not responding to him at all appearing to be in a deep sleep. I pulled the pillows out of the way, grabbed the bottle and picked up the baby. I carried him into the other room, changed his pants and his outfit, fixed him a bottle and sat on the couch with him cuddled in my arms to take his meal. It was a new experience for him and I could tell he liked it. He snuggled right up and took his formula between burps.

Suddenly his Mom appeared in the doorway of the bedroom in an obvious rage. We had been down this road before. She said, "I told you this baby was not going to be spoiled! I do not want him held while he eats!" I gave her one look and said, "You will not treat this child this way in my home! If you don't want to take care of him then we will care for him, too!" She went back into the room and shut the door. The next day she left and it would be several months before we would have contact with her again.

In December I received a clear leading from the Lord that I was to begin the procedure to take custody of the children. But I was to wait. I didn't know why but felt it had to do with the money I did not have. I discussed it with my wife and she was in agreement. We checked with our son and he was certain that this was the right course to take. Time went by and our newest baby made his six month birthday. At that time the Lord moved on me to go forward. I contacted an attorney and came up with $75.00 for an initial evaluation session. He painted a rather ugly scenario for me but I persisted. He asked me the ages of the children. When I told him he said, "Good. They can all be handled in one case. They have to be at least six months old." God knew that. I didn't. That's why He said to wait. He said he would process the paperwork but he wanted $1,750.00 up front to cover the expenses. I left looking at the sky asking God how on earth I was going to come up with the money. He already knew.

That week we would receive a phone call from the paternal grandfather of the oldest child. He heard we had his granddaughter and asked if it would be possible for him to see her. We didn't even know he existed. We scheduled a time and he arrived with his wife for a visit. We informed him fully of what was going on and he asked me if it would be possible for him to go with me to the next appointment with the attorney. I agreed and it was set. The attorney was kind enough to run back through the entire scenario as he had presented it to me declaring that we would probably be in a two to two and one half year fight that would require a good deal of money. I looked at the attorney and said, "No. It will be over quickly. She will willingly sign the papers." The matter of the money was addressed and I said I was trying to make arrangements but had not been successful. The oldest girl's grandfather spoke up and said, "Will you take a check?" I almost fell off of my chair. The full amount was paid. The attorney then said he would be in touch with us but did not want to know where we were. He told me when to contact him. I would find that we had to relocate for a while until the restraining order was served. A place was provided by a member of the family, along with food and gas money so I could get to work and back from this remote location. God was at work. Who could defeat Him?

While this was all in process I had contacted CPS to discuss the concerns we had over some outward actions of the oldest girl. She had been introduced to some unsavory places and we were concerned she had been molested. They would not help us. I can't remember what the reason was. We proceeded with our temporary relocation. I received a phone call at work from someone who was at the oldest girl's school demanding to know where she was. I asked who was on the line and I was told that it was a CPS representative. I still refused to answer the question. I was threatened. I said, "Look. I don't know who you are. I already contacted CPS and they told me they could not help me. I'm not bringing this child over there so you can grab her and run." Now the person calmed down and said, "Do you think that is what is going on?" "You are absolutely correct," I answered. I was given a phone number to call to verify his identity. Once done, I called him back. I then asked him what he wanted and why they had changed their minds. He couldn't answer fully but he said they would investigate abuse charges. There had been some misunderstanding. He again demanded to see the child immediately. I explained why that was not possible and indicated I would present the children at any location he named at whatever time he wanted. We scheduled the next day at their offices in another city near where we were.

We took all three children to this meeting. The oldest child was led away to a question and answer session which lasted about 45 minutes. The younger girl was then led away for about 25 minutes. The gentleman's attitude towards us was very positive as he rejoined us in the lobby. He thanked the children for being so cooperative. He then asked us if we knew where the mother was. I answered in the negative indicating the attorney was trying to find her to serve her with papers. He then looked at us and said, "I cannot tell you anything about the discussion which we had with the children. I do want to know this. Are you prepared to take full custody?" "Yes," I said. "That is what this is all about." He then said they needed to see the mother. There was some necessary drug testing and they had a lot of questions they needed to ask her.

Amazingly, within two days, the children's Mom would make contact with me at my office and ask me where the kids were. I told her they were visiting at a relative's home and would be gone for a while which was true. She then shared with me that she had to be in court the next morning, which courtroom and what time. I never asked. I called the attorney to tell him she had surfaced and where she would be. They served her the papers the next morning.

She did not take the process well but that didn't really bother me. When she contacted me again I advised her that CPS was looking for her, advised her of the interviews that had been conducted with the girls and that she should be prepared for a drug test with some pretty specific questioning. Her response was, "Just bring me whatever papers I need to sign and I'll sign them." She was true to her word. In six weeks it was over and in May of 2006 custody transferred to me and my wife.

Here we were with three little ones again. All parties involved had signed off on the documents and we had a new family to fill in the hours of our old age. We were happy they would be safe and did pray for their Mom that she would one day begin to make better choices. There has been some improvement but to date that has not fully manifested.

The new course for our lives was established. We asked God for the strength to go forward. It was a repeat of a previous scene in our lives as my wife laid her head on my shoulder and we watched the children in their beds sleeping. We had peace in our house again after four long years of stress....and I held her hand.

Chapter 11
DEATH IN A DESERT PLACE

I remember looking up to the Lord at one point and asking, "Why have you brought us here? Did you send us out into the desert to die?" Life in our new land had brought us more challenges than we had ever known before with all of the associated stresses. We had learned through all of this to focus more closely on God and what He was doing in every situation. I suppose that was the glass He had us drinking from. Though the circumstances we walked through were at times crushing, we found a way to keep peace and joy in our inner most being from this time forward no matter what came against us. We had now seen and experienced a lot, especially in the spirit realm, and we had come away stronger in our walk with the Lord. We had found absolute trust in His word and His ways. He had not failed us, though I had accused Him of doing so more than once as we fought these battles. Then He would do what only He could do and I would find myself recanting and repenting once again. My precious wife endured better than I did as she never once wavered from her faith in her Lord. No matter what was going on she would have on a praise tape or CD, have her bible out reading or be found in prayer and praise before God. She was an example to me and I loved her faithfulness. I was the recipient of the blessing of that as her faithfulness to God poured over on me. She was one with my soul.

Every aspect of our relationship had found fullness in God and brought us an intimacy that transcended the physical realm.

The most difficult thing for us to understand was an end to the walk she had been carrying forth for God all of these years. We had stood in complete faith for this miracle. Understandably we had been labeled as less than true followers of Christ over this when we were foolish enough to share the testimony with someone we thought would accept it. We couldn't give a logical explanation for what was happening. We had just taken it on faith expecting that the ultimate miracle of it would be our justification. Our justification, however, would be left to our faith in what God had accomplished through this process. That would remain unseen. This course was complete. My wife sat down with me weeping one day and shared with me that the babies she had carried spiritually with physical manifestations were gone. God had taken them away. She wanted to know what she had done wrong or how she had failed God for this to happen. I did not have an answer, but I did know she had not failed. They were, in fact, gone. We were devastated. Once again we were suffering loss. I was actually angry about it and shared that with God. We had allowed ourselves to be mocked, cursed and a laughing stock to some over this and now there would be no visible miracle. We had even been asked to leave one church though I had only told the pastor and no one else. Why was God doing this? What was the purpose? It was during this phase of our lives that my wife would one day grab my arm firmly, look me in the eye and say, "If I do not make it, do not bury me here. You have me cremated and take me with you. I want to be buried on the land we were promised." I was shocked. I said, "Don't talk like that. We're going to see the promise together."

That is why the next phase of our lives together would be so difficult to understand and remains so even at this writing. Prior to the court process involving the children my wife had begun experiencing an increase in problems with passing kidney stones. It had been a rare occurrence in previous years, but it was something she learned to go through on the days when it would happen. It was a life-long problem. Now, however, the frequency and level of pain she was experiencing was becoming increasingly worrisome to me. She still would not go to the doctor as they had told her long ago that there wasn't much they could do unless the pain was so bad she needed medication until it passed. She chose to tough it out. When she was in this mode I could not even touch her body to comfort her. She would lie prone on the bed until it was over. Sometimes this would last for hours leaving her completely drained.

Things came to a head in 2006 when one of these episodes involved so much pain that I took her to the emergency room of the local hospital. There were x-rays done and she was scheduled to go in for an ultra sound. After reading all of the reports we were told that nothing was found and she would just have to try to alter her diet to inhibit the formation of these stones. She immediately began reducing her calcium intake and made other changes to her diet per the suggestions.

These efforts helped some, but once again we had a serious incident that caused me to rush her to the emergency room. This was difficult for us as we had no insurance. We could not afford insurance and still have groceries for these children we had care of along with all of their other needs. We were not rich people. Once again x-rays were taken and it was reported to us that nothing was found. During our stay whatever had caused the pain had again passed. We could not understand this. In the meantime we applied for charity help for the mounting bills.

Before we could pursue the kidney problem further I noticed my wife was acting a little weak and seemed to be struggling on a daily basis. I suggested we go to the doctor, but she fussed that we already had too many bills for her and she would be ok. She wasn't. One morning she was so shaky I insisted on a doctor visit, made an appointment and we went. She was barely able to walk in and back to the room. When the staff saw her at the check in window they took her immediately to the back, the doctor came in and tests were done. He returned a little later to report to us that my wife was in an extremely anemic state and he was scheduling her in for a blood transfusion. At this point he recommended highly that we proceed with a specialist for upper and lower gastro-intestinal investigations to find out where the blood was going. He was very concerned.

This was going to require up front money or no one would do the procedure. My wife and I were trying to figure out where to get the money as we had no resources. We went home and began the preparations for her scheduled visit to the hospital the next morning. That evening her condition worsened and I again rushed her to the emergency room. I advised them that the doctor had scheduled her in for a transfusion the next morning. They admitted her right away, did the necessary blood matches and began a transfusion. They moved her to a room and I stayed with her through the night. She would have two units of blood administered. We had no less than three doctors visit her room the next morning and each one declared they had car accident victims with more blood in them when they came in and they lost them. We thanked God for watching over her. After the transfusions she was her old self. As we proceeded to check out we were once again in the position of having to ask for charity. The financial officer processed the papers but announced that they had done quite a lot for us so the next time she had a problem she needed to go somewhere else. They would not admit her again since we had no insurance.

Not long after this incident, my wife once again awakened with kidney problems. This time it was really bad. Her right kidney was visibly swollen and she was in horrific pain. I got the neighbors down the street to take our little boy and the girls had gone to school. I loaded my wife in the car and began to drive. I recalled the conversation at the hospital and I sat at a stop sign with my wife laid across the back seat moaning. I had no idea where to go. I shouted, "God! What do I do? I need direction!" I felt that I should go to the charity hospital in downtown Fort Worth. I headed that way and got lost down in that area. I got directions from someone and finally got my poor, suffering wife to the emergency room. It was packed. I tried to make her as comfortable as I could and bugged the personnel more than once about her condition. So much time passed that it was getting near the time for the girls to come home on the school bus. I had no cell phone and no numbers to call. I had to go get them. About that time they came to get my wife and took her through some doors as I went the other way to get the girls. It was a 50 minute drive one way to the house and I got there just before the bus. I secured the girls with our little boy at the neighbors and headed back for the hospital.

Arriving back at the hospital I was allowed to proceed to the area where they had taken my wife. I thought she was receiving care but was shocked to find her laid across folding chairs in an inner waiting area. She still hadn't been seen. I asked if they could provide her something more comfortable and they got her into a larger chair that was cushioned.

Shortly thereafter she was finally put on a bed and transported into the area where she would be seen. She had been in terrible pain now for eight hours.

More x-rays were taken and the attending physician advised us that the right kidney had been hyperextended for so long it was probably damaged beyond repair. It would probably have to be removed. There was a specialist on duty and they were consulting with him. He was looking at the x-rays. We prayed even more than we had been. Somewhere during this time the swelling finally went down and the medication they were giving my wife had effect. She at last had relief. Based on this, they decided to dismiss her but made an appointment for her with the specialist who had been on duty.

Once at the doctor's office more became revealed to us as he looked over the x-rays and ultrasounds that had taken place up to that time. He became visibly angry. He spoke to my wife and said, "Anyone who can read an x-ray or an ultrasound should easily be able to see what is shown on every one of them. You have a birth defect in the tube from your kidney to your bladder. It's probably been there all of your life, but as you have aged the material passing through this restriction in the tube has caused the inner surface to get rougher and close off more making the restriction worse. Every picture shows it clearly. You don't have to be a specialist to see it. You need to have this corrected." We asked when it could be done and how much it would cost. It would cost a lot. He suggested we check into charity help as he would be required by the hospital he was associated with (the one that told us not to come back as it turned out) to sign a document indicating we had a life threatening situation which, though my wife had suffered considerable pain, he could not meet the criteria for doing that. He referred us to a friend of his in another county, which county we happened to live in. He was sure we could find the resources there to help us. He was so compassionate for my wife's situation and our dilemma that he would not charge us for the office visit, which was considerable. We thanked him and proceeded with his suggestion.

An appointment was made with the kidney doctor in this other city and all of the x-rays and other documentation were provided to him. We began the application process for charity help and we would be accepted immediately. The diagnosis was confirmed and surgery was scheduled. A catheter would be run up through my wife's urinary tract and pushed through the restricted area forcing it open. It would have to remain in place for approximately six weeks to allow the tube in my wife's body to stretch out and flow properly. The implant of this catheter was successful and we returned home to wait out the six weeks for the removal. Everything went well and we had no incidents during this time though my wife began to feel a little weak again.

The removal time came and we dutifully presented my wife for the follow up surgery to take the catheter out. The doctor reported after the surgery that the tube held position once the catheter was out and everything looked really good. The anesthesiologist then spoke up and said, "We did have some problems with you during the surgery. We discovered you were anemic and had to administer some blood." I looked at my wife and red flags were waving wildly in my mind. I could see she was scared, too.

The surgeon then said he had already scheduled us to meet with one of his associates in his office. We needed to confirm an appointment and see him as soon as possible to get a colonoscopy performed. The charity we were receiving help from was going to help us with this as well. The appointment was made and the doctor scheduled us for this procedure about four weeks down the road so my wife would have time to recover from what she had just been through.

I waited in the lobby with my wife at this new hospital until she was called back for preparation for the procedure she would undergo. I was allowed to go back once the basics were in place and stay with her until they wheeled her to the surgical suite. Everyone was extremely kind and supportive. We prayed a lot. We were scared.

I waited in the lobby until the surgeon came out. He called me into a side room where in a very stone faced manner he presented me with the pictures he had taken inside my wife's colon. It looked horrible. Yet, I didn't know what I was looking at. Then he said the ugly word. It's cancer. He was actually angry when he said, "This is big enough that it must have been growing in here for at least two years. This should have been caught by somebody. It is pressing up against her kidney, the bottom of her stomach, her ovaries and her pancreas. It has to come out now. If it has attached itself to any of these organs she will not make it, especially if it is the pancreas. It's been in there so long you should prepare for the worst. It is quite large. It is likely it is attached. She's not going anywhere. She will have surgery tomorrow morning. They will call you back to see her when she wakes up. I will have told her by the time you see her."

I thanked him for being willing to help us, but I sat in total shock. I don't know what I was expecting, but it wasn't this. I stumbled back to the chapel at the other end of the waiting area, walked in and closed the door behind me. I fell apart. I wept before the Lord asking, "Why? Why? Why? How can this be? Please, God, help us!" I tried to call my sons and through tears I let them know what had just transpired. I then pulled myself together and went back to the waiting area where they had been looking for me to escort me back to my wife. She was obviously frightened, but she comforted me. "Did they tell you I have cancer? God is with us," she said. "We have works to do for Him, yet. He will take care of me." We still cried together.

Surgery would be first thing in the morning. I stayed with my wife, though I had to run home and make arrangements for the children. The same process ensued the next morning as they took my wife from her room and moved her to the pre-op area. This time I was allowed to go with her. We held hands and prayed. I would wait in the lobby for a little over three hours. I was told to expect six hours or more. Once again I was called into the little room. I have to admit that my legs were rubbery this time but I made it in. The doctor had a little more of a beam about him this time. He reported that the surgery had gone well. It had gone quickly because "the tumor was not attached to anything though it certainly appeared to be in the x-rays". They had removed about a third of my wife's colon and had gotten it all. He had also removed her ovaries as a precaution even though they looked normal as they were the most susceptible for future problems. She needed to be scheduled for preventive chemotherapy. I was flooded with joy. Within the hour I would be allowed into intensive care to visit with her. She was weak but smiling and grabbed my hand. She had tubes all over her with monitors making their usual noises. I leaned over and kissed her forehead, then her nose and lightly brushed her lips with mine. That's about all of the intimacy we had been allowed over the last few weeks and months as her physical body was attacked. Satan was trying to steal our love from us but it was held together by someone who had already defeated him. As stated it went way deeper than the physical. We had a three part love consisting of body, soul and spirit. We were one. God was joined with us and this would not be broken.

Four days into recovery the expected return to normal function for my wife's intestinal tract was not taking place. The surgeon was concerned and decided he had better take some x-rays. They would show just enough that he felt he had better go back in. Something was wrong. We travelled quickly from the height of ecstasy as we were slammed back down to the valley of despair. But we grabbed on to each other and God declaring that this too would pass. This was not an enchanting roller coaster ride. The flesh was being pummeled. The spirit had to stand strong. My wife would have to go through the entire surgical procedure again. I felt so badly for her and I wept on her shoulder because I knew how much pain she had being cut open the first time. She told me she would be alright. God would get her through it.

Once again I waited in the lobby for the surgery to end. It seemed like forever this time. I spent a lot of time in the chapel. When I was called into the little room I was told that a 6" section of my wife's intestine not associated with the surgical area had collapsed. The surgeon had to remove it and sew the two ends back together. She was going to be fine. He had, however, strung about a 30' line through her entire intestinal tract to be sure it did not happen again. I thought he was kidding until the day I accompanied my wife to his office and he pulled it out.

I went to my wife's room in intensive care once again. This time she had a patchwork quilt across her abdomen with holding wires running back and forth across her body. I was informed that this was to hold her intestines in place as well as the "stringer" she now had inside her. Of course the wire tubes that would transmit the chemotherapy medicines were strung all over her insides from the previous surgery. A port for administering the medicine was now prominent above her left breast. She looked at me and said, "I'm so ugly. Do you still love me?" I kissed her cheek and told her how beautiful she was. I never saw her as anything but the beautiful bride I had married though we had gotten older. Of course, I loved her. The anesthesia was still working on her. Then she said, "I haven't been able to be a wife to you for so long. Will you stay with me?" I said, "Sweet Princess. I am not going anywhere.

You're stuck with me." She smiled and dozed off. For the rest of her stay in intensive care I would have to stand near her. She needed to be able to touch me. She needed to know I was there and that I was hers. That reassurance seemed to help her strengthen quickly and she was moved to a regular room. This time everything began to function normally and soon we would be on our way home.

The coming days would involve meeting with the medical facility cancer treatment specialist who would advise us of the effects and procedures involved in administering the chemotherapy. This regimen would involve outpatient trips to the facility where my wife would sit in a chair and the medication would be introduced to the spider web of wires now resident in her body through the port on her chest. Though her tumor had been successfully removed an aggressive regimen was established that would last six months on an every other week basis. A pastor involved in care ministry through the church we now attended would take my wife when I couldn't so I didn't have to miss work. We had actually set under his ministry at another church and my wife's contact with his wife, who had also battled cancer, found us following them to where they were. We had a lot of bills and this help was such a blessing to us. The charity had paid the hospital, the balance of my bill at the hospital that tended to me when I had my stroke as well as my wife's bills there and the bill at the charity hospital in Fort Worth. It was substantial and we were deeply thankful. They did not pay doctors, anesthesiologists, radiologists or other practitioners who were involved.

The chemotherapy was rough on my wife. She transitioned to a portable pack that could be hooked up to her which she would wear for a couple of days as the medication trickled in. If you have been involved in this process you know that the good that is being attempted often carries its own lethal aspects for one's physical person. Toward the end of the six month regimen my wife began to lose feeling in her hands and feet. The doctor had warned of this possibility and told us to advise him if and when it occurred. He changed up the medicine and reduced the concentration for the last couple of sessions. That seemed to give my wife some relief.

The chemotherapy ended and we tried to assume as normal a life as we could. Obviously the treatments had continued to interrupt our relationship as we had once known it and we were anxious to be able to share our love in all aspects once again. We would find to our dismay that the chemotherapy had damaged my wife's internal nerve structure thus taking from us the pleasure we once shared. It would never return to a full normal state. It did not, however, steal the joy that we had in being together and we were thankful for what we did have. My right side had been stolen so I couldn't feel her on that side of my body and now this. We were in church every Sunday declaring our unwavering love for our God. We expected that what had been stolen would be given back to us.

It came time for the follow-up colonoscopy and another surgical procedure. I hated to see my wife go through all of this again but she had to be checked out. This time when I entered the little room off of the hospital lobby I was greeted with, "She has a clean bill of health. I don't need to see you again for a couple of years." Thank God!

We had gotten through 2008 and we were into 2009 rolling right along with good news around us. The next hurdle was the chest x-ray which would take place one year after the end of the chemotherapy. That took place around July and we were called in to see the cancer specialist for the results. The x-ray had shown a small spot on my wife's right lung behind her breast. A biopsy was needed to verify what it was. We were in shock. This couldn't be!

The biopsy was scheduled back at the hospital where she had her surgeries. The surgeon came in and indicated that this growth was in a very precarious position and he was going to put her out as she had to be very still. One wrong move and he would collapse her lung. I waited with her in the preparation area once again until they wheeled her away. I walked as far with her as they would let me. We had been praying constantly. The wait in the small lobby seemed endless. Eventually the door opened to the doctor and nurse who had handled the preparation of my wife for the procedure. The nurse simply said that I could see my wife now. The doctor said the biopsy had gone successfully. I could tell by the look on both of their faces that the news was going to be bad. I tried to smile and shook the doctor's hand though I was now filled with trepidation.

Two days later we sat before the cancer specialist and he gave us the news. My wife had suffered metastasis. The cancer cells had moved from her colon to her lung. The chemotherapy had not been successful in destroying all of the cells. The next procedure was to try to make my wife last as long as they could with various chemotherapy medications. There was no possibility of a cure. They could perhaps extend her life as much as five years with constant medication. We sat crushed just looking at one another. The doctor excused himself from the room.

This time we did not cry. I asked my wife what she wanted to do. I would support her in whatever decision she made. My heart was being ripped to pieces inside. She pulled up her favorite pet name for me. She said, "My Sweet Baboo. I love you so much. Please understand that I can't do the chemotherapy again. It was such a horrible experience. I can't live the rest of my life with that sort of agony. I prefer to put myself in God's hands and share with you whatever time He gives me. He can still give me a miracle of healing." It was September of 2009. The decision was made. We didn't look back.

We drove the twenty five miles home just holding hands. No words were spoken. We now faced the most difficult thing we had ever been asked to go through. It just couldn't be. We had so many promises for the future. We planned to minister together in Florida at some point. It was during the time prior to these tests that it became clear to us that this was where we were bound for. We were looking forward to it. This just didn't fit in. We walked into the house and I walked through the rooms as though I had never seen them before. I was trying to absorb everything I could of life in this place and block the message we had just received from my mind. It appeared my wife was doing the same thing. We ended up sitting together on the edge of the bed. We still hadn't spoken. I just looked into her eyes and she looked into mine. Then I grabbed her and shouted, "No! No! No! This can't be! My heart hurts so badly!" We both fell apart and wept in each other's arms.

The next difficult task was telling our sons. My wife didn't want to say anything to her family right away as the medical side would inevitably come forward in an attempt to dissuade her from her decision. She knew it would be because they loved her but decided to delay it as long as possible. We did have some joy to help offset this pain when our youngest son and his wife presented us with a beautiful grandson near the end of September.

We were advised that the cancer would grow and would probably spread to her spine area next. It did. My wife began to have trouble with her right hip hurting her which was a result of this further cancer cell spread. She had difficulty around Christmas but loved the season so much that she did not want it to be spoiled for anyone. She did not let on the difficulties she was beginning to have. I began to have to balance my new sales manager position with the needs she and the children had at home. I had to assume more and more of the household activities as my wife could not do them. She took over the counter pain medications for a while and that carried us into the spring. We planned a trip to our home state as my wife wanted to see her mother. She constantly prayed for her salvation. She had set at her father's bedside back in 2002 and during that time she had led him to receive Jesus as Lord and Savior. He passed away from cancer at the age of 78 exactly five years to the day after my father who also died at 78. He would be buried on our middle son's birthday on January 21st just as my father had been. She was used by God to lead them to salvation, as well as my mother who passed away in 2008. My Princess was determined to share the plan of salvation one more time with her mother.

We scheduled a July trip and I signed up for vacation time. As spring wore on my wife told me we needed to go in June. She asked me to switch my vacation schedule. I did. We arrived the second week of June at her brother's house in the country. She loved the big old house he had moved out there. She loved the country setting. She had grown up a farm girl. Her oldest sister came to see us and we made plans to go to her home in Omaha before we left. The primary visit took place with her mother at the nursing facility. She was 88 years old and doing pretty well. We had a very nice visit and the kids enjoyed seeing their great grandma again. My wife would reach out one last time to her mother by walking her through her bible showing her the places where it is declared that we must make a personal statement of faith in Jesus Christ. You had to ask Him into your heart and declare Him to be your Lord and Savior. Knowing about it wasn't enough. You had to do it and mean it. Church membership, though admirable, would not be a substitute for personal faith expressed in His atoning death and resurrection. There seemed to be a break through this time. I explained to her mother that this was precisely what her husband had done in his own way and he was in heaven waiting for her. We had to depart without her actually saying a prayer. It had to be left in God's hands.

Our trip to Omaha included taking the kids to the zoo. It was a great zoo but the hilly nature of it began to wear on my wife's hip. She struggled on a couple of the hills and I took her arm and helped her. Her sister began to look at us with deep concern. My wife still did not want to say anything. I held my peace. I did declare that we would have to leave the zoo at one point as she was tired. The kids played the next day in a water spout park located in a park area behind her sister's home. They had fun but it was still a little cool. My wife walked around to where we were and enjoyed watching the kids. She let me know she wanted to go home. We left the next day.

As we travelled home my wife was having a lot of discomfort with her hip so I did not try to make it all in one day like we usually did. It was an eleven hour drive. I stopped about halfway and got a motel room. We would continue on the next day. There was a wild animal refuge in southern Oklahoma that we had always meant to stop and go through over the years but had never taken the time. This time my wife wanted to see it. Since you drove through it didn't seem like a bad idea. The kids had a blast pushing feeding pellets out the top of the windows to the animals that would crowd around the car. It took a while to go through and at one point the car overheated so we had to set for 15 minutes surrounded by animals before we could go on.

Once home my wife began to tend to some duties in the house while I decided to detail our car after the trip. It was a mess. While at it I did my son's car which was sitting there. I made trips in and out of the house for cleaning supplies. It was June 14, 2010. June 4th we had celebrated the 38th anniversary of our blind date. I finished up the cars and went back inside. As I came in the back door I turned to see my wife lying in the middle of the kitchen floor. She could not get up. Her hip had given out. I rushed over and helped her to her feet. I escorted her to the couch and made her comfortable. I was receiving another kick in the stomach but I didn't let her see it. From this day on I would assume all of the cooking and house maintenance duties. She would not be able to do it again.

I remember on three occasions during the balance of this month that I held her in my arms, which I had to do carefully because of her hip, and wept uncontrollably crying out, "I can't be losing you! I just can't be losing you!" She would reply, "You are not losing me. God will take care of me." Her faith was unshakable. Every day she read her bible isolating on the healing scriptures. She repeated them out loud never wavering in her love or faith toward her Father in heaven. June rolled away and July was with us. Her pain was becoming such that I took her to the doctor in a little walker that someone at work had loaned us. They prescribed a stronger prescription medication which would be increased in strength at a subsequent visit. I was now going in to my office late after feeding the kids and tending to my wife's needs. I kept a phone by her and would call her constantly. I took extended lunches to take care of her and the children and left work early in the afternoon. My boss allowed me great flexibility and my coworkers covered for me.

Events quickly advanced to the place by the end of July that my wife could no longer get up and go sit on the back porch, but with help could get to the couch. I could still get her into the tub to bathe her but it was getting harder. As August came around I was wearing out and mentioned to the person at work that had given us the walker where we were as I returned it stating she could no longer use it. She immediately referred me to a hospice care service that had helped them. They would not charge as the doctor who headed it up made the service available to anyone who needed it relying on donations and other methods of financing. Once contacted, the people of Covenant Care became a Godsend to us. They moved right in with oxygen, hospital bed, pain management programs, visiting nurses and employees that would come three or more times a week to give my wife baths and change her bedding. We were treated as though we were the richest people on the face of the earth.

Time was going by too fast for me. I tried to keep busy around the house as I had taken medical leave when my wife became bedridden so I could be at her side. Money came in from my company, fellow employees, relatives and friends that helped me pay bills and prepare for the ultimate outcome of my wife's illness. Our oldest son bought her a television to put in her bedroom as she could no longer get to the living room. I administered her pain medications as instructed and her pain was well managed. Our middle son flew in from Alaska to stay with us and help out. His fiancé came along and took charge of the kids. Our youngest son worked in Fort Worth. He and his wife came out as often as they could with the newest grandchild so my wife could see him. We were drawn together for this hour.

I remember being out in the living room one day when I sensed God's presence so strongly. I began to pray beseeching Him to give us a miracle of healing. One of those television programs had done a "send $100.00 and you will get your healing" scam. My wife always knew better than that but the morphine and other medications were having an effect on her. She called and donated the money charging it to our credit card. I was upset but did not let her know it. That is why I was in the living room praying. I had angrily declared before God that "a little leaven leavens the whole lump. These people are false and need to be exposed. Let them be exposed for who they are." Not too much later a big scandal broke out regarding this ministry.

God had not joined me in my living room, however, to address that situation. He had come to bring me a message. He reminded me in my spirit of a time before I walked with Him when He revealed to me that I would lose my wife. I was shocked. I didn't want to hear it! When I was young this was one element of the fear I had in making a commitment regarding a girl. I felt like I would be passing a death sentence on her. Silly, I suppose, but to a young boy it was a ground shaker. By the time I met my wife I had forgotten about this. Now I had to look at it again. God had known this all along? I fell to the floor in the living room with my thoughts of healing shattered as I heard the Lord say, "I am taking her home. She will be safe with me. She is not strong enough for what lies ahead."

I was screaming, "No! No! No!" I was weeping uncontrollably and crying out to God even as Hezekiah must have asking God to change his mind and give us more time. I began to shout his healing scriptures at the ceiling reminding Him that this was His word to us. We were His. We hadn't been perfect but we had obeyed. He couldn't let this happen! My wife called out to me after a few minutes asking me what was going on. I came in and sat with her my face washed with tears. Again she asked, "What is wrong?" I would not tell her what I had heard. I simply said I was making intercession for her before the Lord and the Spirit had fallen on me. She accepted that and thanked me for praying so hard for her.

Our church came and joined in my wife's bedroom to share praise and worship with her. This was something she missed as she could no longer go to church. She used to love to dance before the Lord. There were those who came that left here in tears expressing the fact that they had come to bless her, but they were leaving blessed by the peace and joy she expressed to them and by the way she had joined in the worship. She insisted that I go on Sundays with the children and continue to teach my class but in late September I was no longer willing to leave her side for that long even though my son and his fiancé were now here. Things were progressing to where I had to assist her more with her bodily functions as they no longer performed naturally. The morphine and other medications allowed me time with her but she wasn't the same person anymore. I was losing her. The growth that had developed above her right breast was now huge. Many people came by from church to pray with us.

During this period she began to see visions of things. I remember her asking me, "Whose baby is that sitting on the floor over there?" There was no one there and I told her that. She was insistent. "You had better look again. He is sitting right there. Who does he belong to?" I said, "I don't know, Princess. Perhaps God is using that gift of yours to show you a future event." A little grandson is due to be added to our family near my birthday the end of this year. Again, she spoke to me with a little anger one day saying, "Are you having an affair?" I was completely baffled. I said, "No, honey. I am not having an affair. What makes you ask that?" "I saw you sitting on the couch with a younger woman with your arm around her. Are you seeing someone else?" Once again I said, "No, baby. You are the only one for me. Maybe you are seeing our oldest granddaughter all grown up and she's finally accepting some affection." She then said, "But I see a little boy and a little girl. Who do they belong to?" I said, "I don't know what you are seeing. Maybe our oldest son will get remarried and have more children." She looked a little perturbed and I attributed some of this to the medication, yet I knew that God had used her like this in the past. Things did come to pass on other occasions that she had seen. I put all of this on the shelf to ponder.

As October rolled around I remember my wife grabbing me by the hand, looking sternly into my eyes and saying, "I am not ready to die, yet. I want to stay and work for the Lord. If I die you lay hands on me and raise me up!" This was an earth shaker for me. I just looked at her and said, "I will do as you ask." Her breathing was becoming more difficult now and the oxygen level was slowly being increased. October 6th rolled around and I found that I needed to monitor her constantly. My middle son and I took turns with my commitment to the night shift. Her breathing would stop and she would have to be tapped to get her to breathe. Somewhere in the early hours of October 7th I passed out. About two hours later I jumped awake and looked at my wife. Everything the nurses had told me to be prepared for was staring me in the face. No breathing, the coloration, no heartbeat, jaw dropped open and eyes rolled back. My wife was dead. I had no idea how long she had been this way. I grabbed her with both hands and shouted her name along with "Come back!" She did. It was the 38th anniversary of the day she finally accepted my marriage proposal.

The amazing thing was that she came back with little or no pain. She started eating, the medications wore off and she was my wife again. I could talk to her and share with her as could the rest of the family. She was so happy. I dared to believe that this was perhaps the start of a miracle. Perhaps God had mercy and the "Hezekiah prayer" had been answered. This would continue for 21 days. We all rejoiced in having her back though the reality of her overall physical condition did not seem to be improving. Yet, again, she experienced little pain.

On the morning of October 28, 2010 my wife suddenly began to lose her ability to speak or use her hands. This was an ominous sign. This was a sudden negative change from the previous 20 day period. Her breathing became labored. I called the nurse who came by immediately. She looked at me and told me to turn the oxygen up. Then she said, "Do you know where we are? Are you ready?" I said, "Yes." It was sinking in. There would be a miracle, but not the one I wanted. I went ahead and sent the kids to school. They were too young to go through this day and I wanted to keep things as normal as I could for them. I returned to the room and my wife tried to converse with me and my middle son who was holding her right hand. She was having trouble forming words. I remember her saying there were three reasons why she could not be healed. I said, "Princess. There is no reason why you can't be healed." She then looked at me and said, "I love you with all of my heart." I said, "I love you with all of my heart." I took her left hand in mine. She then said, "I'm tired now. I need to rest." I told her to go ahead. I would be there with her. She then said, "Jesus. Jesus. Jesus." and closed her eyes for the last time.

It was 10:30 in the morning. I called my son who was an over the road trucker but was in the area and told him to head for home. I called my youngest son. My timing should have been better but I just couldn't quit hoping. I sat with my wife with her hand in mine until 4:00 p.m. The kids came in from school. I called to them and said, "You had better come in here and tell your Nana good-bye. She's leaving us." They came in and the two girls kissed her cheek. Then our little boy, who was so close to her, climbed up on the bed, got right next to her and kissed her cheek. A small tear formed in the corner of her right eye. I squeezed her hand as I sensed a strong spirit and said, "Jesus is coming." I stopped for a moment and said, "Princess. Jesus is here now. I hope He's going to give you back to me, but if He says it is time for you to go, then you go with Him. I'll be ok." At 4:10 p.m. she departed her body and went to be present with her Lord….and I held her hand.

Conclusion

FAITH, HOPE AND TRUST

The necessary phone calls were placed. The nurse came back to our house immediately. Our pastors from Souls Harbor Community Church rushed over and took charge of the house, ministering to us in our grief, bringing food, serving everyone who wanted to eat, handling all who came for a visitation and cleaning up afterwards. Their arms were around our shoulders.

I asked the nurse to remove the tube from my wife's body that had relieved her bladder. I had already removed the oxygen tubing from her nose and the lines to the bed area. The machine was shut down and quiet at long last. My wife was covered only with a sheet as her body's heat generation made any kind of clothing including light hospital garments uncomfortable for her. I asked to be alone with her and closed the door. My son worked with the nurse in filling out the information for the death certificate. I drew the sheet back from my wife's lifeless body and I began to talk to her. I found one of her favorite blouses and put it on her. I found a pair of her favorite matching slacks, grabbed some underpants and dressed her with those. I then placed socks on her feet. I brushed her hair dripping tears on her face which I then kissed off of her forehead, cheeks, eyes and nose. I talked to her constantly throughout this process apologizing if I was clumsy about the tasks I was engaged in. I found her blue covered bible, which was worn from constant use and crossed her hands over it placing it just below her chest. I then placed two chains in her fingers one of which said simply "Nana" from the kids and the other containing a cross. I lowered her head position a little more and stood in utter disbelief that she was gone. I was completely devastated. When she had taken her last breath a crushing pressure had come on my chest that I would carry for three months.

I opened the door to allow visitation. The nurse had contacted the crematorium and they wanted to know when to pick up the body. I told them to wait until 8:30 p.m. My sons were still on the way and the truck driver would need more time to get there. This would be their only opportunity to see their Mom and say goodbye. There was more crying as each one arrived and the finality of our situation began to encompass us. My beautiful Princess was gone. My sons' Mother was gone. My grandchildren's Nana would not be here to see them grow up. The finality was suffocating.

The personnel from the crematorium came to pick up my wife's remains at the scheduled time. I removed the ring from her finger that I had placed there 37 ½ years and one day prior to this time. I slipped it onto my little finger where God had me keep it for another 40 days. She was wrapped in a sheet and lifted to the gurney for the journey outside to the van. One of the attendants kept the sheet off of her face allowing me to walk beside her and grasp every last glimpse of her that I could. They paused at the van and allowed all of us a few more moments to say goodbye. I leaned over and kissed my Princess for the very last time. The sheet was pulled over her face and her body was lifted into the van. I looked at the attendant and said, "Please take special care of her. She has been the joy of my life for 38 years." I watched the van pull out of the driveway and remained fixed on it until I could not see it anymore. She was gone. She was really gone.

A memorial service was scheduled for the following Tuesday to accommodate her family as they were mostly located in our home state and had a considerable drive to get to where we were. All five brothers and five sisters would come with some of their spouses, but her Mother was unable to attend. Again the church stepped up and helped me with a Power Point program of her life with accompanying music, while coordinating every other aspect of this farewell to the one we loved so dearly. Afterward more than one person came up to me expressing the emotion that they had never been to such a powerful service.

My youngest son would accompany me later in the week to retrieve my wife's ashes. I carried her remains home in a paper bag I was given which contained a simple plastic case with a plastic bag inside sealed with her ashes. I would purchase an urn of a simple nature later that was intended to house two. My instructions to my sons are declared to have my remains cremated, remove the two plastic cases one of which contains her ashes now, replace them with a larger heavy duty plastic bag and pour our ashes together in the one bag. It can then be sealed and by then I believe I will have found the place she spoke of where we can have our remains laid to rest. We are going to be busy shouting together around our precious Lord's throne and we won't have need of these bodies anymore!

Time passed and I began to realize that there were just too many holidays, birthdays and special days we always acknowledged together. The youngest son's birthday was the day after the memorial service and we tried to make it special. My middle son and fiancé were flying off to Hawaii. My oldest son would go back on the road and the kids would go back to school. I would be alone. I was so very alone. I did my best to make Thanksgiving what it used to be and cooked all of the special dishes that my wife would always prepare. She had kept me involved in these preparations over the years using me as her "taster, chopper, peeler, mixer, etc." so it was pretty close though the dressing lacked her special touch.

Forty days had passed and I clearly saw a gold chain in a vision with our two wedding rings hanging from it. I did what I felt led to do and purchased the gold chain, attached our wedding rings and hung them around my neck. They would stay there until what would have been our 38th wedding anniversary in April, six months after her passing. At that time I would awaken to the darkness of my bedroom and have a vision of something spinning slowly above me shooting off gold flecks into the darkness of the room. As I watched this object rose up toward the ceiling and was joined by another object spinning slowly and shooting gold flecks. As they spun they began to spin gently around each other. As they neared the ceiling I suddenly realized that it was our wedding rings. A hand that I could not see, though I knew it was a hand, enclosed the two rings. The vision ended. I was instructed to remove the chain from my neck and put the rings away.

The next phase would be my birthday right before Christmas and then Christmas itself. I tried to decorate as my wife would always do so the kids would have the consistency they needed. My heart wasn't in it but I did my best to put on a happy face. New Years was next and the other two son's birthdays followed in January. Mixed in with this cycle I found that all doors were closed to me for getting any help for daycare or babysitting services for the children. My vacation renewed in November and I used up a couple of weeks during the holidays at the end of the year so I could stay home with them. I felt strongly led to apply for early retirement in late November and had done so. My first check would come in February. My oldest son would begin to contribute more to the household needs so we could survive as early retirement barely met the basic bills. I worked through January and used up my remaining vacation to fill in all of the missed hours to keep my paychecks at an accustomed level for bill paying. In February I began a restricted part time regimen to help in the transition of power and assist in training as I looked to the end of my tenure there. That would finally come on April 21st, 2011. I had a pre-k boy and he had to have me home in the afternoons. God was opening only certain doors for me. He knew what was best.

Late in January, having gone through many of the myriads of emotion stated in the foreword to this writing, I came to a time where I didn't have an impending special day to occupy my thoughts on the horizon and the full sense of emptiness that was inside manifested. My son had come home for the weekend and taken the kids out to give me some of the alone time I needed. It was a Saturday as I recall and I was busying myself in the living room cleaning when that crushing in my chest that was constantly there seemed to start to bubble inside me. As this happened, I felt compelled to take out a copy of the Power Point memorial service for my wife which I had converted to DVD for the family and play it. There she was again from the time she was a baby, to when we met, the wedding and pictures taken throughout her life. I sang along with the music and when it ended I looked up at the ceiling and screamed, "Why?!" Everything in me began to come out and I screamed as I cried for over an hour. I was glad our home was in a country location with large distances between homes. I could not handle the pain I was feeling now and I was sure I was going to die from a crushed chest and broken heart.

Near the end of this time I cried out, "God, please help me!" I felt the form of a hand penetrate my chest and in my spirit I saw a hand close around the pain. It was as though I could see the pain as an object and as the hand closed around it I began to feel the pain and pressure being relieved. The hand then withdrew from my chest and the pain was gone. I lay in a limp, motionless form on the floor for a long time, dozing off and awakening later feeling no further sense of the agony that had been my companion since my wife had gone home. This event did not stop those times that came when I would touch something, see something or hear something that would trigger a flood of sobbing and tears. Time has healed some of this, too, but had this been an ink on paper effort there would have been many rewrites to reconstruct soaked pages.

There have been many things that have transpired during this last year but I will recount only two. All of our sons have had dreams with their Mom in them and they have all recounted similar descriptions of her appearing in a younger, more beautiful form than any picture I have of her. She's not wearing glasses anymore, has long brown hair and her skin is as a radiant white light. She expresses her happiness and shares about the wonder of her surroundings. Her mother was reported to have had a similar dream seeing her in the same form (related to me by one of my wife's sisters) to which her mother had said, "That daughter of mine is in heaven." I said, "Of course she is in heaven. Jesus Christ was her Savior and Lord. That's all that is required."

The first of the two particular dreams I will recount involved my youngest son who was approached in a dream by his mother and another young lady. In his dream he asked his mom how she was to which she responded that she was very happy. He then looked at the young lady with her and started to say, "Who is that with you. She looks so much like us." This was a reference to himself and his brother. It came out in the dream as "She looks so much like you." His mother responded with a big smile saying, "This is my daughter." (This was the little girl we lost in a miscarriage just after our middle son and before our youngest son was born. I recounted earlier how I was allowed a vision of her around what would have been the age of 5.) She appeared to be the same age as our sons in the dream. The little ones do grow up in heaven.

My most vivid dream came at another point of transition in my life. We had just had a birthday party for my wife on August 15th. I baked a cake for her as I always did and we all sang Happy Birthday to her. It was one of the last events I had to face during the course of this year without her. Of course I came away missing her terribly again and that sense of loneliness flooded in. Not long after, on August 25th, I had a vivid dream with my wife in it.

We were sitting in a church. There were voices in the distance and the sound of people busily preparing for something. My wife was intent on the proceedings. I was impressed with the fact that she was making sure everything was being done properly and in order. She never spoke. I was sitting to her right watching her intently. This scene seemed like it went on forever in the dream. I knew she was leaving and I had a tremendous sadness but I also realized there was nothing I could do to change it. I then heard the hustle, bustle and conversation of more people in an adjacent room. At that point I reached out and took my wife by the hand and led her to the room from which the commotion had come. We never spoke. Once in the room, I turned and faced her. I looked into her eyes and then embraced her as I placed a gentle kiss on her lips. Our embrace became stronger and I kissed her with more passion. (I had not been able to kiss her goodbye because of her problems getting air.) After a time my wife pulled back from me, took both of my hands and looked shyly at her feet as she would often do when I kissed her that way. She then looked into my eyes and gently, but firmly declared with a smile, "You are going on now." I looked up and realized the room was decorated with numerous red packages with gold trim. I knew it was prepared for a wedding. She disappeared and the dream ended.

Now I look to each day knowing my gracious and merciful God is with me as I travel the course that will one day bring a reunion with the one He blessed me with for so many years of my life. She is there waiting. I've told the Lord to save on some construction materials as I'll be staying at her mansion. I will get there for the same reason she did. I'm not perfect but my Savior and Lord Jesus Christ is and He has made the way for me. I am an expression of faith in His finished work.

I can see the shining light guiding me there already. For now I have a course to run and a race to finish. Give me the strength, Lord God, that I may run my race as well as the precious bride, friend, soul mate and lover with which you graced me. I'll be there soon, Princess. I'll be there soon, Lord. I love you both with all of my heart! I will see you face to face....and I will hold your hand.